There's a Rock on Martin Avenue

by

Sandra Feen and Cliff Treyens

Sandra Feen and Cliff Treyens

Copyright 2025 Sandra Feen and Cliff Treyens

ISBN: 979-8-9890481-9-9

There's a Rock on Martin Avenue

Introduction

This book is about a group of people who meet and have met once a week around coffee and food for the better part of three decades. While it focuses on Wilma Brehm, Bob Brown, Vern Feen, Ray Treyens, and Steve Watkins, it could just as well be about countless other similar groups that proliferate from coast to coast in the United States. We daresay that wherever older people gather to sip, sup, and speak—anywhere around the world—it's the same fascinating gumbo of musings, trials and tales.

If you had a one-on-one encounter with any of the characters in this book, you might not find it memorable. But these men and a gal are proof positive that if you get a person in the company of longtime friends often enough, the ordinary becomes extraordinary.

We assume the overwhelming majority of these coffee clutches are composed of elderly people because they have time on their hands. And if you stick with one of these groups, over time you will see the ravages of aging and how old friends journey through them together.

On a personal level, we can say that this transitional period from the golden years into the end-of-life years is both heart-wrenching and heartwarming. It is heartwarming to see people in their 90s animated, laughing, and loving each other's company. It is heart-wrenching to see them die, one by one, as their bodies and minds progressively fail them. Each stage affords opportunity to experience some of the richest, most profound moments of a life.

In the Bible, a memorial stone was erected to mark a

significant event such as the crossing of the Jordan River by Joshua and the Israelites as they trekked to the Promised Land. Our book title, *There's a Rock on Martin Avenue*, is a memorial stone of sorts, for it has come to represent some dear friends, most of whom are gone. For reasons you will discover, that statement-become-title was uttered literally hundreds of times around our Wednesday Morning Breakfast Club table. It simultaneously signifies American history, the coming of age in a time gone by, shared experience, the bonds of friendship, and joy—so much so that we are periodically drawn back to look at the rock and remember.

As you read this book, we hope you will laugh with these wonderful characters, ponder what they've experienced, and cry at love shared between friends near the end of the road.

Sandra Feen
Cliff Treyens
—December, 2024

Table of Contents

I Birds of a Feather 5
Old Men, Coffee, and a Slice of Life 7
Inevitably Invisible 11

II Profiles in Courage and Other Curiosities 15
My Dad 17
The Unforgettable Vern Feen 25
The Right Stuff 31
The Stuff of Legend 37
The One and Only Wilma Brehm 43
A Ray of Sunshine 49
Into the Season 55
As Fate Would Have It 57
Prologue and into Brothering Season 65

III Predicaments 69
Bob Talks About Getting Tough at Air Force Survival School 71
When the Song Changes 73
Thanks for the Memories 75
Easier to Swallow 81

IV Dirty Old Men and a Gal 83
Imagine Lincoln Owned a Whorehouse and Miss Kitty Approved .. 85
A Sunday Authority 89
Sparring Partners 91

Hokey and the Bandit	93
V Assorted Morsels	**97**
Benevolence of Servers	99
An American Woman's Montage	101
Ash Monday	105
No Other Response Needed	107
Parade Day	109
VI Come What May	**113**
A Broken Record	115
Falling	121
Hospicetality	127
Letting Go	131
Pill Popping and Dropping	137
VII The End of an Era	**141**
Vern and Wilma's Last Tee Jaye's Sunday Together	143
Aside	147
Comforter	151
How to Repurpose	155
Neverland	159
Acknowledgments	***165***
Authors' Biographies	***167***

There's a Rock on Martin Avenue

I
Birds of a Feather

Sandra Feen and Cliff Treyens

There's a Rock on Martin Avenue

Old Men, Coffee, and a Slice of Life
[Cliff]

Truth be told, I viewed Dad's recurring invitation to join him and his buddies at McDonald's on Wednesday mornings with reluctance. I thought of them as geezers, all in their eighties except Dad, the patriarch at ninety. Nope, too busy for that, I thought—places to go, people to see.

Upon retirement in December, 2018, I had no excuse, so I went. After a single hour-long, coffee-guzzling gabfest, I suddenly understood why Dad rarely missed these gatherings. I was alternately delighted, irritated, and at times, speechless. Ultimately, I was drawn into the three-ring circus of six to eight older men engaged in a nonstop torrent of reminiscing, social commentary, poking fun, and laughing at each other.

When these old guys gather, it's like putting on an old shoe—familiar, predictable, feels good. Every week they'd drift in. David was usually first, and Vern, last. Dad *always* got an oatmeal followed by four cups of coffee. Halfway through, someone got a bag of McDonald's apple pies—one for every person except Vern and David, who declined. There's no accounting for taste, or lack thereof.

Try following three to four simultaneous conversations between hard-of-hearing men at a long table in a crowded McDonald's. Once I watched David and Vern, sitting right across from each other, talking about two completely different subjects, their "conversation" unhindered by the fact that neither could hear the other. They chatted on oblivious to their non-intersecting dialogue, and they enjoyed it.

Steve, a Tar Heel by birth, would sit at one end of the long table. He had an opinion about . . . well, everything. That made for lively conversation, particularly with Vern, who sat at the opposite end of the table. Bob would turn down the volume on his hearing aid at times to preserve what hearing he had left. Steve punctuated his pontificating with lots of winking and eye-rolling. In contrast, Vern, a former history teacher, glowered and retorted, armed with historical facts. What a spectacle as Steve and Vern would go at it while the rest roared with laughter! Whether they were worked up or working each other over, coffee at McDonald's never ended badly.

Watching these codgers was like viewing one of those raucous shouting matches in England's House of Commons. I often served as an arbiter, using Google on my phone to settle questions of fact in these hotly-contested, inconsequential debates.

Their faces, like well-worn road maps, spoke of many hard-traveled miles. They were of the "Greatest Generation," spanning the Great Depression, World War II, the Korean Conflict, and Vietnam, on into the massive societal and global change of succeeding decades. Most were servicemen, but they didn't talk much about it other than to share some military shenanigans. To a man, they cared deeply about America—no one more so than the soft-spoken Rudy, whose voice was hardly audible above the McDonald's din. His family barely escaped Germany during Hitler's rise to power. He loved the USA with a passion.

Long retired, they included a shoe salesman, an "arn-worker" (iron worker), a high school teacher, a former jet fighter pilot and aerospace industry employee, and ad salesmen—all hardworking, devoted husbands, fathers, and providers.

These men were characters with character, possessing an esprit de corps through thick and thin. When Mom's health was declining, Bob, John, and wife Joan were there with whatever was needed. When Mom died on Memorial Day in 2017, the McDonald's gang rallied around Dad. Whenever any of them or a family member was ill, hospitalized, or undergoing trials—the guys were there with food, transportation, house-help and, most of all, company.

What bound these diverse old men together? The L word was not thrown around the table unless it referred to a ball team or some sort of food. But one thing is as certain as Wednesday morning coffee at McDonald's—these guys *loved* one another. It's what kept them coming back for more. In an unpredictable world at the twilight of one's life, it's good to be loved.

Sandra Feen and Cliff Treyens

Inevitably Invisible
[Sandra]

—31 October 2021

I played my oldest sister Holly's favorite Monkees album from her junior high years and she started singing into her mascara. We entertained Dad, dancing the jerk, the pony, and the swim, as he labored hard getting into his dress shoes. Dad normally met with a group of church people who typically chose to have breakfast together during the church service hours rather than attend, but this time he requested going to church, and I told the breakfast crew that we'd have lunch for anyone who would like at Dad's, after. Bob, a former pilot and Korean War-era vet, said he'd gladly attend church and the after-lunch. A delightful character, Bob said it was appropriate for some heathens to return to church on Halloween.

Holly told Dad wearing a tie wasn't necessary. This was one facet of Dad's constitution that still remained. He insisted on a tie, just like he never went to work without a suit and tie, and in his thirty-year career as an educator, he only missed two days of work. But what it took to physically get the attire on him . . . .

Some of Dad's favorite people weren't there. They either didn't feel well or chose not to attend. Two of his favorite friends did go to lunch. Holly and I prepared a lot the day before. Jenny made beautiful cutout leaf cookies. Polly talked to Dad the night before about his plans. We drove in separate cars to church so that Holly could leave right away to start heating food. In case Dad wanted to linger and chat with people, I stayed with him.

Bob and Ray went. Again, Bob is a Korean War-era vet and Ray was a World War II vet. At that time, Bob was ninety-one and Ray was ninety-eight! My dad was "only" eighty-eight, but his mind, memory, and cognitive clarity were not anywhere as in sync as these gentlemen's. I honestly don't think mine is either.

Dad tried to keep up with them, sometimes interrupting them or blurting out subject matter that had nothing to do with what they were talking about, sometimes beginning to speak, but then language just plain failing him. More and more, different facets of his life collided. He began a story about the three of them all going, as military men, to see a burlesque dancer on North High St. and he struggled to grasp the name of the place and the dancer. (He once disclosed that gem to a home healthcare worker, but never his family.) I opened my big mouth and said, "Oh Dad, you weren't in the military with Bob and Ray. You were stationed with other servicemen and went with—"

Ray piped in "Oh, you're talking about Rose La Rose at the Gayety, right Vern?"

"Yes. Yes." Dad glared at me. "See?"

Something triggered Dad at one point to start thinking about Mom and he repeated incessantly that she died too young and it was so unfair. His mouth was heavy with sadness.

There was a box of unopened red wine on my mom's kitchen floor for months. (The kitchen was Mom's domain—as were all things home—and will remain so, in my mind.) I had brought it over and my memory wouldn't let me recall where it came from. I asked the gentlemen if they would like a glass, and they all said "Sure," in unison. Bob joked that I provided a classy wine. It took me forever to open the cardboard and wedge the knob out to get the wine flowing, and Ray said World War II ended in less time.

I asked each of them how long they had been married before their wives died: Bob, sixty-one years, Dad, sixty-three years, and Ray, sixty-seven years. I said, "Here's to three men and the success of their nearly 200-year collective marriage record!" Dad seemed to like that.

Bob played with his toothpick, fork, and spoon, and showed us engineered suspension is possible. It was a poignant time together.

I went the next morning to take some supplies over, and to see Holly before she left. Holly said he was extra-slow getting ready because he wouldn't go to bed. She was running late to get back to work in Detroit for a meeting and decided to get online at Dad's. I took care of Dad while waiting for the caregiver to come.

I knocked on the bathroom door and asked if I could come in. He had his pants on without his underwear and I pointed this out. "I think there's too many cooks in this kitchen," he said.

"In other words, it's time for me to get lost, huh, Dad!" And we both laughed.

By the time he came out of the bathroom, he was morose, shaking his head. He said that the "time in church was just awful." The minister who Dad knew well and who had officiated Mom's memorial went to another church. The person who replaced her died. Sunday's minister did not ask during her service if there were any new people there or anyone returning who hadn't been there for a while—"All ministers are supposed to ask this," he said. I was impressed that he noticed she was remiss. "No one talked to me, Bob, or Ray at all," he lamented.

I affirmed that yes, it was not right that she didn't say anything and it was great he noticed, but I hoped it would be of some relief for him to know that four people *did* approach him—that his congestion in his head—as I'd been referring to his illness—merely made him forget, and I proceeded to provide him with details.

"How can you say that? You weren't there," he said matter-of-factly.

II
Profiles in Courage and Other Curiosities

Sandra Feen and Cliff Treyens

My Dad
[Cliff]

Some of my earliest memories of Dad picture him standing tall in a white T-shirt, khaki pants, and a belt with a shiny silver slip buckle. My perspective, that of a tot looking upward. I was fascinated by a silver ring on his right hand with a bomb insignia. More than a decade had passed since Dad served in World War II, but the vestiges of that seminal experience branded him still.

Not yet in kindergarten, none of these things held particular significance for me. All I knew was there he stood—a towering figure, both in stature and in my little heart.

As I reflect on Dad, I realize that there's so much I don't know. Like his father, he never was a talkative person the way Mom was. She could talk with Aunt Betty—or anyone else who would listen—for hours at a time. She would sing "Hello Dolly" at the drop of a hat and twirl around the living room to demonstrate her dancing skills, then talk about the piano and ballet lessons she took as a child.

Dad, on the other hand, was generally a man of few words. His breakfast mates bantered incessantly, words spewing from their mouths every which way. Dad's mouth was not filled with words but with corned beef hash, sausage, and the like. At opportune moments, Dad would spew a few words, sometimes with a bit of egg to boot. When prompted, he could tell a story or two, vignettes really, like when his Great-aunt Kate watched Dad take off on his solo flight at the conclusion of his flight lessons.

"That's the last time you'll ever see him," she said matter-of-factly. Little did she know that Dad would later survive fifty missions as a tail gunner in a B-24 Liberator bomber over Europe and North Africa.

His recollections span the horizon from the tragic to the sublime to the oddly interesting-but-insignificant. There's that time his father, Clifford, took him to watch from afar the horrific Ohio Penitentiary fire on April 21, 1930, when 322 inmates were burned alive; when Dad, a righty, snatched Cincinnati Reds Hall of Famer Tony Pérez's foul tip out of the air with his left hand; his tedious niche jobs at a piano factory; and blowing the little bulbs on glass thermometers.

Some stories were glimpses of Americana—Dad talking about his corduroy knickers that would whistle when he walked as a kid, or how his woodshop teacher threw a board at him for misbehaving. There's the one about his little sister Pat, shrieking with horror, running like a cat with its tail on fire when a locust got caught in her hair; and how swarms of crushed locusts would slicken the streetcar rails so that the wheels would spin in place.

Dad's father, Clifford, and his favorite aunt, Kay, were legendary family storytellers—Grandpa often through his weekly letters, and Aunt Kay in person in her booming contralto voice.

Some of the stories were dramatic. I'll never forget Aunt Kay, not one given to flights of fancy, telling a story about Dad with all seriousness. We sat spellbound as Kay related how during World War II she arose one night, disturbed that something might have happened to Dad. She went downstairs from her bedroom and there, in the dining room, she saw Dad.

"I'm alright, Kay," he said without prompting.

Thing was, Dad was across the ocean in the war at the time. When Kay later told Dad about this, he determined that on that very day his bomber had barely made it back to base from a mission. It could have been his last. Coincidence? We thought not.

If I were on a bomber, there's no one I would rather have my back than Dad. He was *loyal*. After graduation from college, when both my brother and I lived out-of-state, Dad would send us handwritten letters.

What a remarkable contrast to our hurried, abbreviated ways of communicating today. Receiving a handwritten letter from Dad was like getting a piece of his heart in an envelope. I don't mean something syrupy, but something genuine. Most often, he related the everyday things of life, nothing major, but it was a touch of Dad and a touch of home. When we received those handwritten letters, we knew that he took time to think, write, fold the letter, seal the envelope, lick and press the stamp, and then walk it on down to the corner mailbox. Every week. For years.

Dad's affection was most evident by his actions. It seems like just yesterday that Dad, Jim, and I were wrestling on the living room floor. We would try with all our might to pin him, but to my recollection, we never did. Of course, he'd be wearing his white T-shirt and khakis, him grunting and us squealing and laughing with delight. We really thought we could best him, but he was, and will remain, the undefeated champion of the world to us.

In spite of long work days as a display advertising salesman for *The Columbus Dispatch*, Dad somehow managed to make most of our school events. He was there for the spring and Christmas band concerts—Jim on trombone and me on trumpet. Bear in mind that Dad was not a particularly musical person. He couldn't play an instrument, except, perhaps, some rudimentary harmonica. Nor was he much of a singer, though I can remember him singing "The Yellow Rose of Texas" along with Ernest Tubb and His Texas Troubadours on the stereo.

Dad faithfully transported me and my teammates to cross country meets. I loved it that Dad was driving us kids, with us all nervous-like, to the meets and then driving us back as we celebrated victory or nursed the agony of de-feet.

For twenty years after that, Dad and Mom would travel to my marathons and ultramarathons. They were there for my very first marathon in New Orleans. What a sacrifice for them, to go all that way and to not be able to actually watch the race, as twenty-three miles of the twenty-six point two were not accessible as we ran on the Lake Pontchartrain Causeway. They were there for one of my Boston Marathons; they drove, I flew.

But one of my favorite memories is the time they attended my participation in the Old Dominion 100-Mile trail run which started and finished in Front Royal, situated in mountainous northern Virginia, spitting distance from the Appalachian Trail and the Blue Ridge Parkway.

It was my first trail run and, frankly, I didn't know what I was doing. I got lost five times in the darkness of the woods and the Shenandoah River valley—finishing in twenty-nine hours and thirty-five minutes, just shy of the thirty-hour-did-not-finish cutoff.

Dad guffaws telling how he and Mom planted themselves near a dirt road waiting for me to come. Then way down the road they lit eyes on me. They watched and watched, but my progress appeared very slow. When it was evident that I wasn't getting any closer, they moved in for a closer inspection only to realize the plodding son they'd been waiting for, for God knows how long, was in fact a leaning fencepost.

When Mom died, it broke both our hearts. Dad and Mom will always be the picture of an adoring couple to me. They did everything together. Dad would delight in being the driver of the car while Mom was the planner and navigator; I use those terms lightly, as all the planning and navigation took place on the fly in the car. It was that way, always.

As a kid, I remember us rolling into small towns in the middle of nowhere seeing nothing but neon "No Vacancy" signs. Eventually we'd find a vacancy, which often left Mom in tears as she observed roaches in the room and cigarette burns on the sheets. After Jim and I were out of the house, Mom and Dad continued to take these seat-of-the-pants trips and loved them.

Dad and Mom were hand-in-glove to the very end. I remember one day remarking at the clicking sound of Dad's unglued dentures. Then, as if on cue, both Dad and Mom, leaning back in their recliners, in synchronized fashion turned their faces toward me and clacked their dentures like castanets! God, I wish I had had the presence of mind to record that on my phone. I laugh every time I think of it.

To hear Dad tell it, he loved every minute of retirement since leaving *The Columbus Dispatch* in 1988. Of course, one thing you need to know about Dad is that he wouldn't have admitted it even if he hadn't enjoyed every minute of retirement. Dad was a glass-half-full kind of guy. He didn't complain. And when it came to adversity, he was a master of understatement.

One Saturday after Mom had died, I went to Dad's house bringing lunch. As soon as I opened the door, I heard him say, "Look at this!" To my horror, he held up his left hand and his middle finger was about three times the size of the others. I almost puked at the sight. "How long has it been like that?" I gurgled. "Two or three days," he replied. I only found out recently that it was more like a week. Long story short, they had to amputate half the finger due to the infection. He wasn't even sure how it started.

Dad aspired to live longer than his father, his mom (Lucy) and Aunt Kay—all of whom died at age ninety-one. Dad nearly beat the record by a decade, just two months shy of 101. In the final year of his life, Dad was not standing tall physically, but he was otherwise. He still went out with friends twice a week and a third time just with me. Most days, he cleaned his plate, marveling how much food others at his assisted living facility left behind. After numerous falls, Dad finally conceded to using a walker even though preferred a walking stick, hand-carved with a serpent twisting down its length. I would recognize the thump, thump, thump of Dad's walking stick anywhere.

This writing is just a thumbnail sketch of Dad, and a small one at that. There is so much more I could write. Some might say that my parents were ordinary people.

But God says there's no such thing as an ordinary person, and I wholeheartedly agree.

In recent years, I came to know Dad at a different, spiritual level. Every week, I did a Bible study at his assisted living facility. There's that loyalty again— Dad front and center, every time. The number of participants would vary from two to twelve on a given week. But one thing I knew for sure, Dad would be there. When it was just him and me, it was a great time together.

How do you fill a void like that? Well, you can't. I'm just waiting for the day when Mom, Dad, and I can make new stories, sing, dance, laugh, and love together in Paradise. Then it will be a never-ending story, and what a day that will be.

Sandra Feen and Cliff Treyens

The Unforgettable Vern Feen
[Cliff]

Vern Feen. Remember the name. Vern Feen was the stuff of legend, and I can honestly say I will never forget him.

Vern might seem an unlikely legend. He was a bundle of contradictions. His crusty persona could morph in a flash into a cuddly teddy bear. We, his buddies around the Wednesday morning breakfast table who became accustomed to Vern's finger-wagging history lectures delivered with authoritarian vigor, were often on the receiving end of his wilting gaze.

Suffice it to say Vern had more layers than an onion. This once-professorial, long-time public school history teacher emerged from childhood in the Bottoms, a working-class neighborhood in the low-lying community of Franklinton west of downtown Columbus, Ohio, near where the Olentangy and Scioto rivers merge.

Whatever intellectual acumen Vern acquired over the years in the halls of education, his roots were in the haunts of the Bottoms. As he regaled his upbringing, I could just imagine young Vern sneaking around Pappy's Pool Hall, or perched on the hill above the railroad tracks, or playing catch on Meek Avenue. Now, Meek Avenue, that's a good one. I kidded Vern about the irony that *he* of all people could grow up on a street named Meek. Vern loved to hear that, and cracked a smile at every telling.

Vern's grasp of history spanned the horizon. He could tell you at great length about the seminal moments in human history, from World Wars to the impact of US

Presidents, to social movements in the history of America, to the shifting of tectonic plates.

Then, he could delve into obscure, little-known things. Vern loved to ask for a dollar bill, and then with dramatic flair, point out the little banner that says Federal Reserve Note. He had a keen eye, as many have never even noticed that little label. Federal Reserve Note is another name for paper money. Turns out, paper currency in the United States started being issued by the Massachusetts Bay Colony to fund military expeditions. The other colonies subsequently adopted the practice of issuing paper notes. This is but one small withdrawal from the historical bank that was Vern's brain.

Books could be written about Vern, just as Vern could have written books. Why, he had an encyclopedic knowledge of baseball. If you were lucky, after he was done telling you about the batting averages and strikeout records of Major League Baseball players going back to the 1800s, Vern would reminisce about his playing days as a kid, and as a pitcher at a small Ohio college. In terms of stature, Vern could not have been an imposing figure on the mound at the height of five-feet-and-some-change.

"I didn't throw fast, but I had a good curve ball," he said matter-of-factly.

There was so much more to Vern than that. He was a devoted husband to his bride, Rae, and they shared sixty-four years together before his better half passed away in 2019. Vern and Rae were proficient at producing lovely and successful girls. Of this Vern was undeniably proud, more than ever as they doted over him in his golden years.

There's a Rock on Martin Avenue

The Wednesday morning breakfast table wasn't the same without Vern. He never disappointed in instigating "discussion," telling it like it was, and wagging his finger to punctuate the numerous points he was making. Life without "His Meekness," as I sometimes called him, has been diminished.

I noticed an interesting thing at our Tee Jaye's Country Place breakfast table on Wednesdays. Our loud, often animated, and sometimes raucous conversation drew a crowd. You could see patrons tilting their heads toward our table to catch some of the action. Smiles would crease faces as patrons caught fragments of our banter. It was like the sitcom *The Golden Girls* in front of a live audience.

One week I saw a guy seated in a booth about ten feet away sitting opposite his wife, tuning into our table. When he could stand it no longer, he called out to Vern.

"Did you used to teach at Starling?" he asked, his excitement palpable.
"Yes," said Vern's daughter Sandy.
"Did you drive a blue Rambler?" said the man, now halfway out of his booth, eyes glued on Vern.
"Yes," said Sandy.
"Did you used to drive around looking for boys who were skipping school?" said the man, who at this point could barely contain his delight.
Vern acknowledged that yes, in fact, that was he.
"You used to chase me around the neighborhood in your car!" the man said, bursting with joy.

At this point, the rest of us were totally drawn into this man's memory, picturing Vern hunkered down over the steering wheel, hands in the ten-and-two positions, eyes scanning streets of the Bottoms like radar, looking for wayward boys.

Somehow, as only Vern can, his former days as the Starling policeman engendered genuine affection of this former juvenile fugitive. Why, thanks to Vern, this man was now a convert to the notion of vigorous enforcement of the law.

"I think they ought to bring the paddle back!" he exclaimed. You could sense that this man, who fifty-plus years ago was running for his life from Vern in his blue Rambler, wanted Vern's approval. It was priceless.

Now, those who are deemed to be worshipped breathe rarified air. I looked up "worship" in my *Webster's Third New International Dictionary, Unabridged*. On page 2,637 it states this—"Worship: The reverence or veneration tendered a divine being or supernatural power." Now, Vern's picture is not next to that definition, but it might as well be.

This is not empty talk, I tell you. Daughter Sandy was actually teaching at Starling not too many years ago. A student there, upon hearing the name Feen, made the connection that Sandy was related to Vern. The student was dumbstruck and star-struck vicariously through Sandy. His response to standing before her was reminiscent of a knight dropping to his knee before a queen.

"My family worships Mr. Feen," the student said. "You have to come to my house." Well, this was weird, as it was not every day that a student invited Sandy to come to his/her house a.k.a. a place of worship for her dad.

There's a Rock on Martin Avenue

With some trepidation, Sandy agreed to make the visit. Upon arrival, the student guided Sandy into the living room. There, on the mantelpiece, were two framed pictures. Sandy's eyes just about popped out of her head, her mouth agape. The first framed picture was of Vern. The second was the Creator and Sustainer of the Universe; that is, Jesus Christ. No joke. Vern was being worshipped on the mantel with Jesus a.k.a. God, in the flesh.

I could go on and on about Vern. But there is one thing that must be mentioned, for it has come to symbolize the place Vern has in our hearts.

You see, there's this rock on Martin Avenue in the Bottoms. Vern brought this up every time we met at the breakfast table. In fact, he brought it up more than once at every breakfast. Eventually, I had to see this rock— and I did.

As rocks go, it's no Gibraltar. It's about four-to-five feet high and three-to-four feet wide. It is situated at the end point of a grassy median separating Martin Avenue into two roads. A bronze plaque commemorates a treaty that was signed during the War of 1812.

I will never forget that rock because of Vern Feen. And when I think of it, I will not think about the War of 1812 and that treaty. I will think of Vern, the boy scampering around the Bottoms, the teddy-bear history buff who has given countless hours of delight to so many people, the finger-wagging, salsa-dancing wonder of which there will never be another.

If it were up to me, I'd replace that plaque on the Martin Avenue rock with a testimonial to Vern Feen. Why, I'd name the whole street after him. This legend deserves nothing less.

The Right Stuff
[Cliff]

In my mind's eye, I have this vivid scene of a man strapped into the cockpit of a blazing-fast jet aircraft. As he pulls back the throttle, the cockpit begins to shake, the instruments vibrate, and light outside the canopy begins to distort and bend. As the velocity increases, a quivering needle nears milestone speed.

The aircraft begins to shake so violently that disaster seems inevitable. And that's where the vision ends.

If this sounds familiar, it should. It's an iconic scene from the movie, *The Right Stuff*. Funny thing is, it's not Chuck Yeager sitting at the controls in my daydream. It's Bob Brown. That's right, Bob Brown. And the needle is quivering at Mach 1.06.

Not all this story is imaginary. Bob Brown has flown Mach 1.06. That's 813.3 miles per hour to be precise, fifty-two miles per hour faster than the speed of sound.

The other odd thing is that in this vision, Bob looks exactly like he does now—probably because that's the Bob I see at our Wednesday Morning Breakfast Club. He's ninety-four years old, aviator glasses pressed against his face, leather flight jacket, and fighter squadron ball cap resting atop his balding pate. It's a tight fit in the cockpit for ninety-four-year-old Bob, but nevertheless there's the old man streaking through the heavens.

Bob Brown is an extraordinary man with an ordinary name. He's regularly mistaken by mail carriers, government bureaucrats, and law enforcement officers for one of the countless other Bob Browns out there.

This Cold War-era jet jockey has the right stuff. When he begins to tell a story, one of two things happens—either everyone quiets down to hear his soft voice or everyone talks over him because he has a soft voice.

Hearing is a problem for Bob. In fact, hearing is a problem for everyone at the Wednesday breakfast table except Vern's daughter, Sandy. The rest of us are afflicted with poor hearing that ranges from moderate to nearly stone-deaf.

Bob has one of those cochlear implants. While he has to fiddle with the newfangled thing from time to time, there are some advantages. The Bluetooth option is handy for answering the phone; and when things get too loud at the restaurant, or if he wants to tune out insufferable conversation, Bob removes the ear pieces, slams them to the table and, ah, sweet silence.

Clearly, no woman could ever replace Bob's beloved wife, Ruth. That said, Bob has been known to have a lady friend. We guys are always clamoring for juicy details but, Bob, always the gentleman, never tells. About the best we can do is try to judge his moods. As a matter of fact, one of those 70s mood rings might be a good affection meter for Bob.

Bob used to sweet-talk the Southeast Asian manager at McDonald's—the McDonald's we formerly used for breakfast. He knew only a few words of her language, but that was enough. Just about every Wednesday, Bob would trot out those few words, and she'd give Bob his food for free, or darn near it. In fact, she was so enamored by Bob that I'd sometimes get my food for near-free just because I sat with Bob. There we'd be, happy as clams, sipping our coffee and munching on our hash browns, Egg McMuffins, and hotcakes in the shadow of a life-sized fiberglass Ronald McDonald, marveling at our silver-tongued tablemate.

Speaking of eating, it's been a challenge for Bob to keep up his normal eating pace and diet. Over the years, we've witnessed his teeth disappearing one by one until finally, last year, they were gone and he was fitted for dentures.

This was the beginning of another saga and some of the best news fodder we've had for years. Every week we'd get an update on the progress of his dentures. You see, Bob was beset with problems getting those darn dentures right. Whether it was his mouth or the dentures, Bob looked like toothless Snuffy Smith for what seemed darn-near six months.

When they finally got the dentures right, it was quite a day. Bob was happy to pop them out and give us a good look-see. But we digress.

Bob is a reservoir of great stories, too many to recount, which often flow from his military experience. One of our favorites is the time during survival training that he and some other guys trapped, killed, boiled, and ate a porcupine. Unlike the listeners, material like that never gets old.

Then there was the time Bob was out on the town in South Korea when he missed the bus back to camp. Apparently, missing the bus in Cold War Korea is something you do not want to do at all costs. Then there is the story, or stories I should say, about the time Bob was chosen to be the real Chuck Yeager's right-hand man on Yeager's temporary assignment to the then-Lockbourne Airforce Base outside Columbus, Ohio. Apparently, Chuck not only pushed the envelope in a jet, he pushed the envelope in about every way imaginable, including calling meetings around a meeting table without chairs, requiring everyone to stand for the duration of the meetings.

Sure, these are good stories. There's no denying that. But they pale in comparison to the Mother of All Stories. It's so delightfully outrageous a story that I've retold it dozens of times. This episode involves his wife, Ruth. It's classic Dagwood-and-Blondie or Lucy-and-Desi stuff. In this case, it is Bob who is impaled on the horns of a dilemma. Even now, when the story is mentioned in Bob's presence, he looks heavenward and apologizes to Ruth.

So it goes that one day, Ruth decided to do a good deed for her dear husband, Bob. While he was out, she figured she would take his favorite jacket to the dry cleaner. Ruth made sure to check the pockets. Bob's jacket had lots of pockets, as you might expect of a flight jacket.

After Ruth cleared all the pockets one by one, she noticed a small pocket on the upper sleeve of one of the arms. She reached down in there and felt a little, inconspicuous something. She never, ever, in a million years would have imagined what came out. Rolled up tight in a little square package was what Australians call a "dinger" or a "franger;" Jamaicans call them "boots." But back in the day, Americans called them a "rubber," or by its proper name, a prophylaxis—that is, a condom!

There were no witnesses to this event, but I think it's fair to say Ruth's jaw must have hit the floor and her eyes darn-near popped out of her head.

Sometime later, Bob innocently comes home, opens the door, and there stands Ruth, arms crossed. By this time, her expression had changed; she was glowering at him like a Catholic school nun ready to whack him on the knuckles with a ruler. I imagine Bob's reaction was not a Cowardly Lion kind of fear but more of the confused-like look of the Scarecrow whose straw brain is trying to sort this situation out.

Ruth surmised that Bob had some use for that condom that did not involve her. In actuality, she was right. As when Lucy got herself into a pickle, Ruth's look conveyed Desi's Spanglish rebuke, "You got some splainin' to do!" I can just imagine Bob bending over in feigned laughter at the misunderstanding, winding up to "splain" himself only to look up and see Ruth tight-lipped, steely-eyed, and about to blow her top.

Perceiving the seriousness of the situation, Bob said in a very rational, Bob-like way that the reason for the condom in that little pocket is in the event he got lost in the middle of nowhere with nothing to drink, and needed to transport some water by storing in that efficiently packed rubberized canteen. "It's as simple as that," I can hear Bob saying.

What Bob didn't realize is that to a normal human being, that is the silliest thing ever heard. I grant you, one might learn this little trick in military survival training, but the chances of a middle-aged Bob trying to survive in the wilderness behind enemy lines with nothing to drink is about as likely as Vern doing stand-up comedy, or Steve dancing ballet.

That's not a plausible story, except for a right-stuff military guy like Bob. Eventually, Ruth came to see that the idea of Bob having an affair was less plausible than him wandering the neighborhood drinking water out of a rubber. So they patched things up, and lived many more happy years together.

There are many things that could be said about Bob that are laudatory, and one very relevant one in light of the last story, is that Bob is loyal with a capital L. He was always a loyal and devoted husband to Ruth. He remains loyal to his children. He is loyal to his friends. I can't tell you the number of times he's helped Ray with rides when he needed to go somewhere, or has checked on others of his friends when they needed help.

Bob is the right stuff because his heart is in the right place. You could go around the Wednesday morning breakfast table and, I guarantee you, every one of us to a man and woman would say, there's no one we would rather have fly our jet at Mach 1.06 than Bob Brown. And so, Bob, we salute you! May your teeth fit properly, may your hearing be sharp and your love overflowing, may your belly be satisfied, and your canteen, always full of water.

The Stuff of Legend
[Cliff]

In my opinion, the term "legend" is thrown around too lightly these days.

New superhero movies come out every week. The Rock and Roll Hall of Fame passes out legend status like Halloween candy, including to people like Dolly Parton ("legend" she is, "rock" she ain't). Today's legend is like yesterday's quiche, which, I might add, real men don't eat anymore.

If you're like me, hankering for a real living legend, I've got two words for you: Steve Watkins. That's right. Shout it loud and say it proud—*Steve Watkins!*

Don't let that folksy façade fool ya. Beneath his southern twang, beyond all that winking and eye-rolling (Steve's favorite facial expressions) is a bona fide, all-American legend. He's like a pentathlete of legendary-ism. Let me break it down for you.

Salesman par Excellence

Let's face it—salesmen are braggers by nature. But talk is cheap. The proof is in the pudding as they say. When it comes to legendary salesmen, the numbers are relatively few, and Steve Watkins is one of them. Why, Steve could sell a glass of water to a drowning man.

Steve was a shoe salesman. No one knows the ins and outs of a shoe like Steve. Vern disagreed with almost everything Steve said, but on this Steve and Vern were of one accord. "Steve knows shoes," Vern said in all seriousness, jabbing his finger for emphasis.

Steve, in fact, is a lot like a shoe, metaphorically. He has eyes, as does a shoe. He can be a heel when he wants to be. Steve's got a soul/sole in there somewhere. He definitely has at least one toe. And oh my, yes, Steve most assuredly has a tongue which wags incessantly at our Wednesday morning breakfast outings.

Steve's dream come true would be for Imelda Marcos to walk into his shoe store with a suitcase of cash. Paradoxically, Steve has single-handedly told off and dispatched countless customers or employees who didn't measure up to his standards. How anyone with those assets could pull off a career in shoe commerce I don't know, but Steve did!

Steve would probably be a shoe magnate by now if shoe knowledge wasn't so undervalued today, and the internet hadn't put most salesmen out of business.

Athletics

To look at him now, you wouldn't imagine that Steve was a world-class athlete, but it's true. Honest. If I've heard it once, I've heard a thousand times how Steve scored perhaps the most miraculous touchdown in high school football history. It is a priceless story that deserves retelling.

Back in the 1950s, Steve was a lankly teenager and a defensive player for his high school football team in Durham, North Carolina. One fall Friday night, his team was doing war against a worthy opponent in the city championship game. At a fateful moment, trailing by few points, his coach, who went by "Coach," looked in desperation for inspiration. His eyes lit on Steve.

"Watkins, get in there!" he barked; the surprise in Steve's voice as he tells the tale is just as evident today as it was sixty-plus years ago.

What happened next was a blur. The opposing quarterback took the hike, Steve broke through the offensive line, and, jumpin' Jehoshaphat, the quarterback stuck the ball in Steve's gut. Then, as Steve tells it, he ran faster than a scalded dog down the field while Coach ran alongside waving his arms like a windmill yellin' "Run, Watkins, run, dammit!"

And run he did, right into the end zone where he collapsed in a heap, only to be picked up and carried aloft from the field by his team. But that's not the best part. Young Steve, already a legend when it came to courting and sparking with girls, discovered that his stock rose considerably among the choicest girls around. Sweet memories they are, even to a legend like Steve.

Meaner than a Junkyard Dog

Back in the 1970s, Jim Croce immortalized the song, "Bad, Bad Leroy Brown." As the song goes—

"He's . . . the baddest man in the whole damn town . . . and meaner than a junkyard dog."

Well, Leroy Brown would be just a water boy for Steve Watkins. To be honest, the details are sketchy as Steve has so many stories about telling off and beating up other people that it all sort of runs together.

Basically, it goes like this—someone disappoints or provokes Steve, then Steve gives them a chance to recant or apologize. If they don't, Steve gives them a tongue-lashing or pops them in the nose. Unlike Bad, Bad Leroy Brown, who gets into a fight and ends up looking "like a jigsaw puzzle with a couple of pieces gone," Steve says never lost a fight. Ever.

Provocateur

As a provocateur, Steve is without peer. The term PC (politically correct) is not in Steve's vocabulary. The most outrageous and sometimes offensive things come out of Steve's mouth, and he feigns ignorance at the predictable adverse response from his senior, elderly tablemates. Steve is a relatively young 'un at eighty-four years of age.

Sometimes, when he's about to say something objectionable, he'll lower his face to the table, look both ways, and mouth the words in hushed tones so as not to verbally assault any patrons, present company excluded. Most of these things are not printable, and are harder to swallow than one of the long, stringy pieces of gristled ham sometimes served up at breakfast. Steve crosses every line imaginable; of this, I need say no more.

But we've learned that if you take what Steve says with one of the countless grains of salt that litter our tabletop, Steve's provocations can be endured with relationship intact.

Friend

The funny thing about legends is that we need them. Sure, inherent in the term "legend" is the notion that a legend is "historical although not entirely verifiable," this according to *Webster's*. Who cares? If telling the same ridiculous story over and over and over were a crime, we'd all be guilty.

Steve is a part and parcel of our little Breakfast Club. If he weren't there, we'd miss him terribly. He is a piece of Americana. Like the rest of us, he represents a living, breathing part of history that is fading fast. When Steve's gone, we won't see the likes of him again. So, week in and week out, we will enjoy the man, the legend, Steve Watkins.

Steve has told me with a wink that he'll someday greet me at the Pearly Gates, as he likes to call Heaven. When I greet him, both of us in our resurrected bodies, there are many things I could say to Steve as a glorified human being. But there's one thing I want to say because I want to see it for myself.

"Run Watkins, run!" I'll shout as I watch him gallop in the End Zone of all End Zones. What a day that will be when legend becomes reality.

Sandra Feen and Cliff Treyens

The One and Only Wilma Brehm
[Cliff]

"I do not like green eggs and ham."
—Dr. Seuss

Wilma Brehm, as they say down South, was "a hoot." You never knew what was going to come out of her mouth, but you could be pretty darn sure what was not going in it.

Wilma, a newer addition to the Wednesday Morning Breakfast Club, made something quite clear at the outset—she didn't like the food at Tee Jaye's Country Place.

From the T.J. Scramble to the Country Ham Special to the Western Omelette, Wilma ordered food only to proclaim it inedible. Sure, she'd never even tried the Hen House Special or The Barnyard Buster or Your Ol' Favorites, but sure as the sun rises in the east, you could bank on her gag response.

Only Vern's daughter, Sandy, rivaled Wilma in food persnicketiness. Meanwhile, the rest of us ate like cows at a trough.

Until I get Alzheimer's, and maybe even then, I will not be able to erase from my mind the picture of Wilma holding aloft a yard-long slice of ham held together by rubbery bands of gristle. The look of disgust was priceless.

Sandy cleverly started ordering for Wilma and telling her that she loved the same meal the last time. It seems to work . . . for a while.

It's hard to believe, but true—Wilma grew up in the Hilltop neighborhood of Columbus' west side, just a stone's throw from the Bottoms where Vern and Ray lived as kids. What are the odds that three coots like these with a
combined lifespan of 280 years came from the same stomping grounds? I don't know what kind of fertilizer they used on the west side way back then, but it sure did yield a bumper crop of characters.

Wilma was a self-described tomboy who played baseball and was constantly getting into mischief, yet nonetheless developed a fondness for boys at an early age. While she didn't play baseball anymore, her fondness for the opposite sex continued unabated after a period of grief following the death of her husband, Harold. In her final years pushing ninety, if you were male and within arm's length of Wilma, you were more than likely to get hugged, kissed, or pinched.

I'm not kidding.

But let's get back to "you never knew what was going to come out of her mouth." An innocent statement about the weather, the news, or some family matter might have elicited a racy comment from Wilma. She was a sly one, too, because when she made those comments it was downright impossible to tell if she was serious or not.

Even at ninety-one, Wilma had a zest for life. Turns out she was an instructor in ballroom dancing for many years. That's one way to ensure you're in a man's arms as much as possible.

In fact, she met Harold at a YMCA dance. Only Wilma could have told you whether she was swept off her feet, but she should have been. Harold was shot on Normandy Beach in the invasion of all invasions that marked the beginning of the end of World War II. He was awarded a Purple Heart. I'm sure Harold would have modestly claimed he failed to dodge the bullet, but the Normandy Invasion was a brutal bloodbath in which nearly 37,000 ground forces were killed.

Married more than fifty years, Hal and Wilma went on to adopt their lovely daughter, Lori.

When Harold died, Wilma's ballroom dancing days ended, but Wilma didn't need a ballroom floor to dance. Put her on any piece of real estate under any circumstances, and she turned it into a dance. Why, not long before her death, Wilma dragged Vern out of his chair at the assisted living facility and did a few twirls around the linoleum floor to "How Great Thou Art." Admittedly, it didn't hurt that they both were very hard of hearing and probably thought they were dancing to "Moonlight in Vermont."

One thing Wilma did stop doing was driving, which was understandably hard and a blow to her freedom. It probably didn't help that Wilma let her sporty red car roll into the garage door. She then joined Ray and Vern in the *Driving Miss Daisy* club, getting chauffeured around, participating in the parade of rollators in and out of Tee Jaye's every Wednesday.

There's a dear picture of Ray, Vern, Bob, and Harold with their wives, respectively, Jean, Rae, Ruth, and Wilma. Wilma was the last of those wives standing. Those who say the men usually go first got it wrong this time.

We're glad Wilma was with us long enough to join the Breakfast Club. First of all, she was hilarious. The outrageous comedian Phyllis Diller had nothing on Wilma. Secondly, she brought her own woman's touch to the table. Wilma was literally a color palette—like fall leaves contrasted against the drab winter landscape of the men, except for Vern's bright red flat cap.

She feigned objection when I likened her appearance to Jean Harlow or Marilyn Monroe. Personally, I'm convinced she secretly liked it.

But the reason we really loved Wilma around the breakfast table is that she was a sweet soul. I can hear her now batting away that compliment, but it's true. When you looked into those beautiful eyes, you could see it. And when she put a sympathetic hand on Vern or Ray, it showed. Jean, Rae, and Ruth were sweet souls, too, and Wilma was a reminder to us of those days.

We're so glad for the time we had with Wilma. If there's

a mold to be broken, God broke it with the one and only Wilma Brehm.

Sandra Feen and Cliff Treyens

A Ray of Sunshine
[Cliff]

The Greek philosopher and physician Hippocrates was a keen observer of people. He peeled away layers of that most perplexing of creatures—humans—to discern categories of behavior.

Little did he know he'd help unlock one of the keys to understanding Sandy Feen, who, in addition to being the daughter of our beloved Vern Feen, is one of the newest members (and perhaps one the last) of the Wednesday Morning Breakfast Club.

Hippocrates categorized all people into one of four temperaments reflecting bodily fluids, of all things. The Choleric has excessive yellow bile, he proffered; the Phlegmatic, too much phlegm (this is literally and figuratively accurate of yours truly).

Though I'm no doctor or philosopher, my diagnosis of Sandy reveals a blend of the remaining two temperaments—the Sanguine with rich, warm blood, and the Melancholy, with dark bile. This is not an insult; no, no. The world would be a bleak and tasteless place without the "San-Mel." Let me explain.

Sandy showed up in 2021, when Vern needed a ride to the Breakfast Club, and it was like the clouds had parted and rays of sunshine came streaking through. The mere presence of a female at the table livened things up, but that's not all. Right away it was apparent that Sandy brought something to the table that was lacking. It was as if the heart monitor went from an occasional spike to throbbing heartbeat.

When she first appeared at our breakfast club, things became . . . well, more fun. Her Sanguine squeals of delight punctuated our gathering, and her eyes locked like tractor beams onto whoever was talking to as if it was the most important and interesting thing ever said. Like a good politician working the crowd, Sanguine Sandy makes whoever she talks with feel that he is the center of her attention.

Author Tim LaHaye in his book *Spirit-Controlled Temperament* says this about the Sanguine:

The Sanguine "is the warm, buoyant, lively, and fun-loving temperament . . . <with> a tendency to lift the spirits of everyone present by <their> exuberant flow of conversation."

This is so true of Sandy. On his 100th birthday, she asked Ray his secret to a long life, which evoked his famous and well-worn adage, "Good genes and not hanging around with old people." Though she had heard this more than once, Sandy cackled with delight at Ray's proverb as if for the first time.

It's been highly entertaining to have Sandy at the table because Steve and I love pigtail-pulling, earning me her title of "the brother I never had" and Steve's faux-mean looks. Steve's countrified provocations punctuated by winks and taunts are like a corn pone food fight.

Steve loves ordering Sandy around, barking at her to pass the salt and pepper, put syrup on Vern's pancakes, or give him one of someone else's birthday cupcakes (which she often brings before, during and after someone's birthday because she simply cannot not make birthday cupcakes). Sandy feigns offense at Steve's chauvinist bravado and then zings Steve right back.

Speaking of cupcakes, my favorite Sandy cupcake is the famous, or should I say infamous, "floorboard cupcake." In spite of her excellent driving, she once managed to maneuver her car in such a manner as to send the cupcakes flying off the seat. The carrier lid, having popped off, resulted in the iced red velvet cake delicacies rolling around on the car floor. This was of little concern to us. To my 100-year-old dad, the carpet fibers were a dead ringer for sprinkles. The misshapen cupcakes looked just dandy to Ray and he devoured two of them lickety-split. The rest of us quickly followed suit, amending the three-second rule into a two-and-a-half-hour rule.

Of the Melancholy, LeHaye wrote: The Melancholy "are the analytical, self-sacrificing, gifted, perfectionist types . . . . It is almost impossible for them to hear a sad tale, observe the tragic plight of another person, or listen to sad music without weeping profusely."

Indeed. Why just last week, after laughing her head off about something, Bob mentioned that he had made arrangements for Vern's lost hearing aids to be replaced. As he explained, tears rolled down Sandy's cheeks and her lips quivered with gratitude. You can't fake that. I'm just saying.

One aspect of this temperament that strikes uncannily true is LaHaye's description of the Melancholy's eating habits: "They are very picky eaters." That seems an odd observation, until you observe Sandy at the breakfast table. Sandy is a vegetarian at a bacon-and-eggs breakfast joint who detests any kind of meat and will not even eat plants violently rooted from the ground. Once the kitchen failed to get all the sausage out of her omelet as ordered, to which she meticulously picked out crumbs of pig and distanced them to the side of her plate. She could barely disguise her disgust.

When you combine the Sanguine with the Melancholy, you get Sandy. LeHaye says the San-Mel make excellent teachers, are people-oriented individuals who contribute to others, and are dreamers. Why, how did Hippocrates know that Sandy would become a teacher, an altruist, and a poet?

At times she can be a little bit clueless in an innocent kind of way, like her doppelganger Sally Struthers in the *All in the Family's* character Gloria, Meathead's wife. Her perplexity often manifests when she tries to decipher one of Steve's malapropistic mixed metaphors.

It would be very unfair and unbalanced were I to focus only on Sandy's temperamental qualities, for the intellectual level of our breakfast table increased exponentially when Sandy joined us. Sandy and father Vern are the brains of the table. In fact Sandy was a published poet even before this book; she is, at this time, the Ohio Beat Poet Laureate. (We had to explain to Steve that a laureate was not a rope you throw at a cow.)

But there is one thing you must know about Sandy. Her kindness, compassion, and heart are just what an old man needs in the twilight of life. We men tend to button up feelings inside and talk about superficial things. Sandy helps us stop and smell the roses, talk a little kinder, and love a little better.

Were it not for Sandy's gushers, the only tears we would ever have seen at the breakfast table would have been those that welled up in Ray's eyes when he talked about his departed bride of sixty-eight years, Jean.

As Vern declined in the months before his death, Sandy would privately share the depth of Vern's struggles and hers. This gave the rest of us an opportunity to grieve vicariously with her.

When Vern died, no one would have blamed Sandy for bowing out of the Breakfast Club. But that's not Sandy. She would experience acute FOMO (Fear of Missing Out). Besides, like me, this unlikely gaggle of old men grew on her. So, she remains a regular at the table—loving us up, and shunning hog jowls and fatback for a grilled cheese sandwich and our company.

For that, we are most grateful. Sandy is a ray of sunshine and the sauce at our table. Things wouldn't be the same without her.

Sandra Feen and Cliff Treyens

Into the Season
[Sandra]

"Walk with me down Woodette!" I plead
on a day flecked with pale yellow,
orange crunch, beige blush of autumn sighing.
This time, you agree. Our goal, the house of my
third-grade twin friends, halfway down the street.
Your walker weaves through maple leaves,
a three-house extension, to the home of friends
I met when I was four.

We share unspoken
amazement you've taken us this far,
while I remain behind you,
observe how your black shoes and black walker
paints you into this autumn landscape:
leaves and pant legs, a unison of color and wrinkled
texture.

This walk canvases a year ago.
How much better
you've handled decline
than I have, as the sidewalk of your mind
continues to gray, narrow, crack.
"Every day is a good day," you say.

Today we eat breakfast at Tee Jaye's
with friends you've known for decades.
Wilma shares the congestion in your head,
bids you to hold up your syrup pitcher
to hers, wants to make a toast.
"Let's salute each other's syrups, honey!"
and together you laugh, unaware of all the sticky
sweet on the sides of both your hands.
Not a minute later, she lifts liquid sugar again,

repeats alluring toast with her wink
and you lean your pitcher to hers. You'll keep
up this ritual, again and again, both the happiest
at the table.

As Fate Would Have It
[Cliff]

"There is many a boy here today who looks on war as all glory, but, boys, it is all hell."
—William Tecumseh Sherman

For a man, war service is a milestone—a life marker against which time before and time after is measured. Whatever excitement and visions of glory exists on the front end of service are ultimately replaced by grim reality of war's carnage on the back end.

I never had that experience. I'm glad I didn't experience war. Yet, I have to admit my heart is drawn to the idea of risking my very life for something bigger than myself. As concerns war, I can only imagine what it would have been like through my dad, Ray.

History sadly lays bare that the "war to end all wars" was not. Barely two decades after it ended, World War I was eclipsed by a larger and bloodier World War II. Some 400,000 American military personnel died, and 38,000,000 civilians perished. More than three-quarters of a century following its end, Ray at Tee Jaye's Country Place was a living relic of that conflict—still operable, if dinged up a bit at 100-years-old.

It would never have occurred to the folks at Tee Jaye's that this man with thinned hair, craggy face, and silver stubble—stooped over, shuffling slowly along over his walker—was once a 6'1", 190-pound tail gunner in a B-24 Liberator heavy bomber. While smaller men were preferred, Ray served where needed—crammed into his tiny turret at the butt-end of the aircraft like "Spam in a can," as the Mercury astronauts used to say.

At Tee Jaye's, Ray was still crammed into a small place of his choosing—his back against the knotty pine paneling and his chest nearly pressed against the large circular table. Getting seated in place was no less an easy task than in his service days. It required wresting the chair back and forth with hand and foot, while he provided hand signals like a runway director. He was more like gristle in a can those days.

One can't really appreciate Ray and the surreal nature of air warfare without eyeballing the aircraft first hand. There is only one B-24 flying anymore, and that four-engine war machine made a visit to Springfield, Ohio in spring, 2023.

Ray made the trek with his friend Bob, a post-Korean War jet fighter pilot—two tottering, hard-of-hearing warriors wanting to hear those big engines rumble one more time.

What happened upon Ray's arrival was reminiscent of Moses crossing the Red Sea. The crowd parted to make way for the venerated old airman with his WWII ball cap. When the B-24's crew got wind that there was a genuine former B-24 veteran present, Ray was whisked onto the tarmac for an up-close view of the airplane. Crew members jostled each other like school boys to take a selfie with the ol' man. Though Ray shunned the spotlight, he nevertheless politely answered as many of the questions his failing ears could hear.

It's a leap to imagine this man, humbled by the years, as a nineteen-year-old firing two 50-caliber machine guns as enemy fighter aircraft strafed his airplane from above and below. Despite the passage of time, Ray remembered it as if it was yesterday.

He enlisted on October 28, 1942; he didn't even have to look it up. That very same day, he shipped off from Ohio to Fort Thomas, Kentucky, then a few days later to Atlantic City, New Jersey, for basic training.

At any other time, Atlantic City would be like an amusement park with cotton candy, carnival games, rides, and beachcombing. But war changed everything. Said Ray, "We drilled on the beach, and everything was blacked out at night. At times we could see smoke from the beach as German subs were hitting American ships."

A month later Ray was off to Armament School to learn how to handle explosives, including the 500-pound and 1,000-pound bombs dropped by B-24s, which had a normal 5,000-pound payload but a short-range maximum of 12,800 pounds.

After that, it was off to Gunnery School in Laredo, Texas. Before long, he was assigned to an operational unit, the 376th Heavy Bombardment Group. The group consisted of four squadrons of fifteen B-24 bombers. He was first stationed in Benghazi, Libya; then Lecce in southern Italy, around the heel of the boot.

The 376th was unique in that it was the only American heavy bomb group activated in overseas combat. It was the first American unit to bomb "Fortress Europe"—the part of continental Europe occupied by Nazi Germany— and the first group to be based on the European continent.*

It was a pioneering group, and at nineteen, Ray was one of the many boys in it who instantly became men. One of Ray's pilots, Mel, was the old man of the group at about thirty.

When asked, Ray casually mentioned that he completed fifty missions. Even one mission could be a harrowing, lethal experience. The B-24 was a formidable aircraft with a range of 3,000 miles. The B-24 was therefore a choice target for German antiaircraft flak and German Messerschmitt fighter planes.

"The versatile 88mm cannon was Germany's main heavy antiaircraft ("flak") gun during World War II. When an 88mm projectile exploded at altitude, it sent out jagged metal fragments that tore through nearby aircraft. It also left a characteristic black cloud hanging in the sky." [Wikipedia]

If that wasn't bad enough, what Dad never told me was that the B-24 was nicknamed the "Flying Coffin." Louis Zamperini, former Olympic runner and POW survivor in the Pacific theater, wanted to be assigned to a B-17 but was sorely disappointed to be placed on a B-24. Zamperini said the B-24 was like flying "an old jalopy." It wasn't long before he went down in his B-24, adrift at sea on a life raft for forty-seven days with two other crewmates, only to land on the Japanese-occupied Marshall Islands. Imprisoned in a horrific POW camp, Zamperini's story was immortalized in the book and film, *Unbroken*.

Not only was the B-24 difficult to fly and didn't perform so well at lower altitudes, it had one exit at the rear of the plane that was all but impossible for most of the crew to reach with a parachute, thus its moniker, the Flying Coffin.

Frankly, I'm lucky to exist.

As a child, I was fascinated with Dad's war experience.

He had this old ammo box, Army green with a metal clasp, full of little treasures. He would open the lid of that box and pull out the most interesting things. One of my favorites was a glass tube with various layers of volcanic ash from Mount Vesuvius, which, by the way, erupted while he was stationed in Italy.

Then there is the story about the time Mom was rummaging around in that box only to find a love poem Ray had penned . . . to someone else. She couldn't really get jealous though, since Mom and Dad hadn't even met when it was written. It turns out that he was sweet on an Italian girl and put pen to paper to express some of his *amore.*

Even to this day, that ammo box contains a little, twisted piece of metal. If you didn't know what it was, you'd be inclined to toss it in the trash. It turns out that little piece of metal was the closest to death Ray would ever come. Some flak tore off a piece of his turret and whizzed by in a hair's breadth of Ray's head. "A little closer and I'd have been dead," he deadpanned.

His first mission was on October 1, 1943—the bombing of a ball bearing plant and depot in Wiener Neustadt, Austria, near Vienna. According to that city's tourism bureau, "Wiener Neustadt was almost completely destroyed by bombs during the Second World War. Around 50,000 bombs reduced the old Babenberg town to rubble and ash."

But one mission of the fifty stood out in Ray's memory—the bombing of a German railroad marshalling yard in on December 28, 1943.

"We went out and missed the target, though we did kill a

lot of ground troops," he said. When the 376th went back a second time two days later, "They were waiting for us. They had seventy-five fighter planes and we had no escort." At the end of the mission, the group lost ten out of seventeen bombers and a total of 100 crew members were forever gone.

"Surely frightening," I ventured. "Not really, no more than usual," Ray said. "You always thought you'd come back. The guys who thought they were not coming back were relieved of duty. They didn't hesitate to make their feelings known. Actually, it was pretty calm. You weren't keyed up but keeping busy."

On another mission, Ray shot down a Messerschmitt fighter plane that was streaking through their bomber formation. I asked him what it felt like to take another life. "I didn't feel very much. That's what you did," he said.

Frankly, there isn't much talk about the military at the Tee Jaye's breakfast table on Wednesdays. Wilma's husband, Hal, who died years ago, was a two-time Purple Heart recipient who stormed Normandy Beach on D-Day. Among the most patriotic of the Breakfast Club was Rudy, also deceased, who barely escaped the *Hitler-Jugend* (Hitler Youth) organization as an immigrant fleeing Nazi Germany. Ray was the last remaining combat veteran among them.

Bob, one of the breakfast gang, just missed out on the Korean War, although he was stationed in Korea for a time as an Ohio National Guardsman. Still, as I hear Bob talk about flying Mach 1.06 in his jet, I sit in awe thinking of him in his cockpit hurtling through the heavens.

There's a Rock on Martin Avenue

Vern was in the Army in a non-combat role in the 1950s. As a teacher, he could have gotten out of it, but Vern considered it his duty to serve, so he did. I've seen pictures, and both Bob and Vern cut a dashing figure in their military attire.

For the Breakfast Club soldiers, their one big wingding was the Veterans Day-gather at the Nutcracker Family Restaurant in the countryside east of Columbus. Many of the old warriors donned ball caps with their war of service emblazoned on the front—from the Gulf War to Vietnam and Korea. Only a few WWII vets hobble in these days. Mostly they go to cash in on their free breakfast and gab about aches and pains, ball games, and days gone by. All around them are a garrison of wooden nutcracker soldiers.

Ray said he was "ready and willing" to go back for another tour, but the war ended before he could. But his war experience would come to play a more enduring role in his life than he ever imagined. After Mom died in 2017, he stayed in his house for a while but eventually moved into assisted living.

As my brother and I were going through the house, we happened upon a piece of paper in Dad's handwriting. Someone, probably the minister of our church, must have asked him to give a testimony.

"I did not grow up in the church. My family were believers, but in my younger years I did not attend church regularly. During World War II, when violent death or catastrophic injury were daily possibilities, I attended services from time to time and believed that in all circumstances God's will prevails," he wrote.
"I can't say that at any particular time I had a 'great

awakening,' but I have professed Jesus Christ as my Lord and Savior."

Nearly four decades later, I made the same decision having struggled through some life battles of my own. Until his death, I went to Dad's assisted living facility to conduct a Bible study and he'd always be there, front and center. We're both in God's Army now. I can't wait to muster with Mom and Dad in Heaven in that time when war is no more and the lion lays down with the lamb.

As fate would have it, war is hell, but for Dad, that's not the end of the story. The best is yet to come.

*From *The Liberandos: A WWII History of the 376th Heavy Bombardment Group and its Founding Units* by James W. Walker

There's a Rock on Martin Avenue

Prologue and into Brothering Season
[Sandra]

—*for Cliff*

You were seven, holding on to the edge
at the start of the deep end of Swimland,
Whitehall's eastside pool,
inching your way to deeper water,
guided by desire to follow older sibling.
Your brother and his friend splash just ahead
as any kids would do, in heat reeking
of chlorine. Your outer landscape, light pink
wooden lounge blocks for sunning, and shouting
happy children, but within—your hand

slips, you're then bobbing in water yelling
HELP, take most nefarious
plunge. Swimmer steps on your body
at pool's bottom, calls guard who reacts, ascends you

to gasp of air, angel's spark igniting you back,
reinserting you to your eight millimeter's frame,
beginning film of your life work—
that summer of '62,

season of my wading in amniotic fluid.
A different pulling planned for late autumn
intended to be less daunting

from a mother readying
herself for me, readying life of books
and braids and songs and prayers; dolls and sisters and
everything girl, churching me just right

to eventually bear thickest muddied waters without her,

to prep me for longest single day seasons—
days in daze—grueling longest goodbye of my father,
her six-decades mate.
And yet.

And yet. Once upon a time when I was four
I danced The Mamas and the Papas'
"Words of Love" with Mom on the living room's
blue braided rug, stopped midway,
asked—as declaration—why I didn't have a brother,
she sang response, "You'll have yourself a brother one
    day,
one day, when you need one most,"
to rhythm and tune of the song.

And I arrive in Dad's men's group
fifty-five years later at Tee Jaye's
and you baptize me in as a member.
You, who first rings my attention
when you bellow Dad's name a verb:
"Have you been Verned today?"
and I see how the audacious magic of your question
makes his facial gloom splinter into flecks of sunshine.
You feign a fresh interest in every story and
phrase Dad repeats, and when his words are
such strange stones or his language defines drought,
you rattle breakfast silence with greater absurd—
"What is bra spelled backwards?"
Another dish of quiet and stares.
Your matter-of-fact response, "Why, Arb."

As Dad's dementia causes a head congestion
that parches, I current further into the sticky wet
of depression, then receive just the right scripture
from you, a text that elevates. Suddenly
"Words of love, so soft and tender"

There's a Rock on Martin Avenue

in that clear Mama Cass tone melodies instant recall,
just as a mother and daughter dancing together
trickles poignant memory, just as here and now,
you brother me through such deep seasons
of laughter, of love, of weeping, and lift me
from drowning.

Sandra Feen and Cliff Treyens

III
Predicaments

Sandra Feen and Cliff Treyens

Bob Talks About Getting Tough at Air Force Survival School
[Sandra]

—*Bangor Maine, 1953*

Sometimes we had to capture our own food if we wanted
to eat, so we made wire traps, and
practiced shoot-outs with a 22.

If an animal crawled into a snare, another movement—
even a quiver—created an instant coil,
snapped its own neck, but then

a porcupine surprised us. He went through, stopped,
still as our hunger stayed. Our dilemma,
how to remove him from the trap without
his counterattack. So we

gunned him inside the wires with a 22, knowing
shooting success imminent with a bullet capable
of 2,000 yards' travel.

We skinned him in a pot
and boiled and boiled and boiled—
we even ate his legs.
He was the toughest to chew.
We might as well have eaten a rubber ball
or the soles of our boots.

Sandra Feen and Cliff Treyens

When the Song Changes
[Sandra]

Lori and Sandy graduated high school together,
share an additional elementary backdrop—
accordion lessons at Columbus Academy
on East Main, juxtaposed to the Lavender Pussycat,
and third-grade choir at Shady Lane
Presbyterian, singing "Morning Has Broken" in
the Sunrise Service, Easter
bonnets and white gloves intact.

Sunday breakfast at Tee Jaye's brings them closer,
bonding in parental loss and navigating
remaining parents' hourglasses of memory.

Today, Lori and Wilma follow Sandy and Vern
to Ashford for a personalized tour
of Vern's living quarters, after Wilma wandered away
from home into the eastside front yard of another facility.
With purse on arm and a Kleenex packet inside
stuffed with important numbers
ready for any angel finding the lost,
Lori receives a call, and Ashford tour begins.

This surviving pair already entered the realm of
disintegrating filters, after decades of friendship
between them and their spouses, who
already moved into the Final Room, where all is restored.

Today, walkers stroll into the bright white light
of the Bistro, otherwise known as the cafeteria
and happy hour spot for geriatrics.
"So does this mean we'll be sleeping together?"
Wilma directs her question to Vern, with her
drizzle of laughter following.

"Oh my God, Mom!" Lori bellows,
bold like a seasoned soprano hitting a
high C. Sandy remains silent,
studies the apple cheeks of her father
growing redder, his smile wide,
mustering up all the focus he can.

Thanks for the Memories
[Cliff]

Based on my experience, the "oops moments" of life start to really ramp up in middle age and accelerate apace as one advances into the golden years. You know those moments, when an accident or faux pas happens. During an oops moment, the protagonist is invariably taken by surprise and the victim/onlooker is caught unaware.

An oops moment can be inconsequential and forgettable, like the countless times Ray and Bob wore food on their faces or clothes. We took those in stride by discreetly motioning toward the egg, gravy, or sausage clinging to their visage or shirt. Other times, these foibles stick in your mind like white on rice. Try as you might, you can't erase those tapes from your memory.

Some oops moments are physical, like the time Vern poured coffee instead of syrup on his pancakes. Other oops moments are verbal, like the time I inadvertently toasted my brother and his first wife—at his wedding to his second wife; or the time I called my second wife in frustration by the name of my first wife. I specialize in ghastly oops.

Here are two choice oops. On a serious note—these vignettes are not meant to embarrass anyone because, as they say, shit happens to us all.

The first episode involves Ray, my dad. It is our practice to look the other way when someone has an oops, that is except when it comes to Steve. We love to draw attention to Steve's abundant verbal oops, because Steve lives for conflict. When you poke at Steve, he grabs onto it like a dog trying to wrestle a stick away from you—shaking his head back and forth, growling, and wagging his tail at the same time.

I think we can agree that dentures are very useful things, particularly when you are missing teeth. They can, however, present problems since—unlike our natural teeth—they have no roots. Imagine what would happen if a tree had no roots. The whole thing would flop over like a domino at the first strong wind.

I remember the time a local TV newsman was doing a live broadcast when suddenly his dentures popped out on camera. As the camera held steady, he ducked down, popped them back in and finished his report. A classic oops, indeed.

Along those lines, Dad's dentures were, well, there's no other way to put it—loose. Very loose. When he talked, the top set would drop, and he suddenly sounded like the Dick Tracy character, Mumbles. At that point, you had one of two choices: either nod your head like you understood what he was saying, or ask him to repeat what he was saying. More often than not we'd nod our heads because nearly all his conversation was garbled due to his unfettered dentures.

Occasionally, I'd ask him, "Why don't you glue those things in?" He'd respond, "I've tried. It doesn't work." In the last ten days of his life, I asked if he was willing to try an adhesive because the hospice nurses were having trouble understanding him. With his permission, I got the highest-rated denture adhesive on Google. He tried it and, eureka! "This stuff works pretty good," Dad said, nonchalantly—that, after twenty years of slipping and sliding.

Anyway, one morning at Tee Jaye's, in between bites of corned beef hash, two eggs sunny side up, and some sausage patties, Ray started to speak when his chops—top and bottom—shot out of his mouth and clattered under the table. Nary a word was uttered. I think I may have shouted, "Three-second rule!"

Anyway, Bob, showing a limber deftness to which we were unaccustomed, snatched Ray's grinders off the floor and handed them below table level to him. Finally, breaking the awkward silence, I asked Dad, "Why don't you glue those things in?" which he ignored. We then proceeded to eat, gab, and mumble the morning away.

The next episode involves Vern. While I'm told Vern was more cantankerous in his younger years, I saw more of his prickly side when I first joined the group at McDonald's years ago. By this point he was one of the most-chill people I knew. Vern usually had a smile on his face at Tee Jaye's, and we worked hard to keep him engaged with us as his dementia increased.

Another thing that increased was a certain lack of control, if you know what I mean. In his final years, these incidences could be quite problematic. As we all know, when you have to go, you have to go. This presented a problem for anyone at Tee Jaye's because the tables were arranged like an obstacle course. Only the most adroit or athletic person could get to the restroom in time. Being a steeplechase runner would have been helpful.

To complicate matters, Vern moved very slowly. As time is of the essence in these situations, the odds were against Vern.

Sure, you have to go when you have to go. But at some

point you don't know when you have to go, and you just go.

One morning, Vern shuffled off to the restroom with Sandy following. She lingered outside as Vern attended to business. After what seemed an interminable time, Sandy asked the manager's permission to enter the men's room. What Sandy found cannot be described in these pages. But, as many of us children of older parents have found, when mom and dad get really old, you often find yourself doing things you never thought you would have to do.

And so she did.

In spite of these problems, Sandy persisted in bringing Vern to breakfast until it was no longer possible, and we persisted with her.

We've found there's is a new normal when our parents near the end of their lives. At first, you do what you have to do, however unpleasant it might be. But hopefully, eventually, you come to realize something far more profound. If you're fortunate as Sandy and I have been, it dawns on you that there is a certain honor in serving your parents, including in the most difficult ways possible.

Taking a lowly position and serving our parents is love expressed in its purest form. I think of Jesus washing the dust and dung off His disciples' feet the day before He was crucified. He was showing them, and us, what real love looks like. We sacrifice, we suffer, and in that we are blessed.

So, I don't want to erase those tapes from my mind. No way. I want to cherish the memory of the oops and the privilege of being there when my parents needed it most. After all, that could be me.

Come to think of it, that is me. I've been oopsing my way through life for sixty-nine years. I've already had an accident after drinking a laxative tea called Smooth Move. Things moved too smoothly halfway between the living room sofa and the bathroom. I was so horrified I disposed of my undergarment in the trash can by the gas pumps at the local convenience store. I didn't want the evidence on the premises at home. Really.

Oh, the silly things that we do. What else can I say except, thank God there were no witnesses, and . . . oops!

Sandra Feen and Cliff Treyens

Easier to Swallow
[Sandra]

Dad meets friends at Tee Jaye's on East Hamilton
twice a week. The waitresses know
he won't veer from his black coffee, short stack
of pancakes, garnish of bacon.

Last Sunday, he poured his coffee onto the stack
instead of syrup. Didn't know the difference.
He prefers to pour, but I wished
I hadn't put syrup so close to his cup.
It didn't matter.

No one really comes for the food anyway.
Words become harder
for Dad to digest,
as well as pass-at-the-table. It's Wednesday;

Cliff asks him his favorite Christmas song.
"Obama," he says, without delay.
Somehow this is an easier thing to swallow.

Sandra Feen and Cliff Treyens

IV
Dirty Old Men and a Gal

Sandra Feen and Cliff Treyens

Imagine Lincoln Owned a Whorehouse and Miss Kitty Approved
[Sandra]

It's Men's Group Wednesday.
Dad's breakfast at Tee Jaye's. I was baptized
into the group, as they verbed it, long ago.
Even Dad approved.
Steve, self-professed flirt from Durham
and Lyndon Johnson's doppelgänger,
always savors a shock, begins today's
conversation with a jolt:
"I'm gonna build me a whorehouse.
I'll call it 'Jump On Me.'
Put that in your book, babydoll,"
and he tugs on my left sleeve
as swiftly as he blows me a kiss.

Korean Conflict pilot vet Bob is absent
from this crew since duty calls him to work
at a pharmacy today.
His eye rolling and groans
would have immediately ensued.

"Lincoln!" Dad yells saluting his middle finger.
"Lincoln!" he repeats.

"What about Lincoln, Vern?"
came the calm but commanding
low voice of the World War II vet,
almost six months to age 100.
If everyone's best memory cells
were collected in one Mason jar
with a golden birthday bow for Ray,
he'd chuckle, politely decline,

not needing at all or wanting
any assistance from any of us.

As if to fill in Dad's
it-should-be-so-damn-obvious blank,
he does it himself:
"Owned a whorehouse."
Table silence.
Dad slaps a glare at me, says
"You heard me," then returns to the group.
"Lincoln owned a whorehouse.
And I'll tell you something else.
He ran it with Miss Kitty.
On *Gunsmoke*. And she approved."

"Miss Kitty from *Gunsmoke.*"
Ray made a declarative statement, then
almost simultaneously held up
his empty coffee mug,
virtually mouthing the word *waitress*,

and Dad responded a matter of fact "Yes,"
as if the 1960's cowboy drama was a place, say,
in the neighborhood of Gettysburg.
A little nervous giggle splashes among the seats,
and Ray's son Cliff dishes out a face of compassion
towards me I so intensely felt, that I fumble,
drop my napkin.
"You, Think. I. Don't. Know.
I know my my my Presidents.
I know my American his . . . his his
hissssssss his HISTORY!" and he nearly growls
the word once he is able to hunt it down and kill it,
then as if an afterthought, a deliciously full sentence.
"I've always been the resident historian."

There's a Rock on Martin Avenue

And that fact is now history.
He curves his middle finger, leans in, stretches
his arm to table's center as if to hook a synapse
of reason in any of us, or even better,
our imagination.

Sandra Feen and Cliff Treyens

A Sunday Authority
[Sandra]

"Eat it and beat it!" Vern yells randomly over the table, middle finger touting his repetitive phrase—a favorite slogan from an old, sorely missed, tiny diner with plates of food nearly as big as their few tables.

"Yes, Nancy's Diner—a great one in Clintonville, now gone," I remind him.

"No. Rose La Rose," Dad replies in thorough disgust, then announces to Steve, Ray, and Bob. "And you all knew her!" His middle finger accentuates his words as if he is pressing a period on each of their chests.

"No, Dad, only Ray. Steve hadn't even moved from Durham yet, and anyway, Rose La Rose doesn't own the diner. She—"

"I'm telling you, they all knew her! And you—"

"Who the hell is Rose La Rose?" Steve breaks in, emphasizing the word *hell* as if his mind directed his vocal chords to follow the word with triple exclamation points. Bob is silent, and I suspect uncomfortable, since he dared bring his girlfriend Donna to breakfast and she just announced that she typically is in church at this time. Ray, wordless, repeppers his eggs, then taps his mug on the table, a signal to me that it is time I refill his coffee mug—coffee I bring in a thermos and hide under the table—since no waitress can pour fast enough.

I mutter under my breath to only Steve, who sits next to me, "Steve, we've talked about her many times. She was a burlesque dancer."

"I never ever saw her," Steve yelps. I wasn't here to see no *Columbus* girl," with a feast of girls elsewhere implied.

Donna quietly adds and asks, her hands folded just below her pink flowered print blouse: "Nancy from Nancy's Diner is my friend. I've known her for decades. Now just who is Rose La Rose?"

"A stripper!" Ray's voice bellows, then he beckons Steve to pass the jelly. He continues, says with conviction, "Vern and I are the only ones who knew her." Ray looks directly at Vern and Vern smiles with supreme satisfaction, his finger now at rest. Ray continues, "I'm sort of an authority on strippers. In fact, I thought about writing a *striptionary*—a stripper for every letter," he says matter-of-factly, evenly spreading jelly across his wheat toast. Donna is quiet.

Bob suddenly veers into a detailed story from his pilot days that he flew Tony Randall, while Ray asks me for another refill. I accidentally pour over the mug rim, spilling a substantial amount on the table. Wilma, who has been unusually quiet, laughs and says to me, "All this talk about a stripper has gotten you excited, honey!"

Wilma's daughter Lori inquires, "Did you fly any strippers, Bob?"

"Not while he was flying," Ray immediately responds.

There's a Rock on Martin Avenue

Sparring Partners
[Sandra]

I know how to protect a man. Just put him behind me.
Can you hear me? *Wilma*
    How can I not hear you? *Cliff*

We'll be laughing our asses off. *Cliff*
    Wait a minute. Let me look. It's still there, honey.
        Wilma

Take my husband, please. *Cliff*
    —And somebody did. *Wilma*

He took you to the woodshed. *Cliff*
    You should have given him some Purell. *Wilma*

I liked my coffee hot, like my men. *Wilma*
    Oh, I thought you meant black. *Cliff*

First of all, I've been famous. I'm over it.
20 or 30 years ago? How old do you think I am—90?
    Wilma
    Well, 91, to be precise. *Cliff*

I liked the snorkeling. *Cliff*
    Did you say snuggling? Well, come here, honey!
        Wilma

I love how lush the landscape was—
the environment in general. *Cliff*
    Well, I'd love to have your curly hair. *Wilma*

What happens if your push this button? *Cliff*
    Not much, darn it! I keep praying. *Wilma*

Sandra Feen and Cliff Treyens

There's a Rock on Martin Avenue

Hokey and the Bandit
[Cliff]

You'd never know it by looking at him, but Burt Reynolds has nothing over Steve Watkins. Well, maybe something in terms of looks. But when it comes to the substance of the matter, Steve Watkins has something over Burt Reynolds.

In the movie, *Smokey and the Bandit*, Burt (Smokey) was bootlegging beer. Steve, on the other hand, was a bootlegger in the real thing—you know, hooch, moonshine, white lightning, mulekick. Burt was simply acting. But Steve—and he swears it on a stack of Bibles—was literally running for his life.

Now, a disclaimer is in order. Whenever talking about Steve, one must take some of what he says with a grain of salt. In the stories I'm about to tell, there is some independent verification of facts. Jeanette, Steve's wife, can testify as to some chase scenes—at least the parts before she shut her eyes and buried her face in her lap. You probably could still find her fingernail marks in the dashboard, but "that hot rod is probably done been blowed up by now."

Steve, to put it plainly, was a bagman in a bootlegging operation. I suppose it's called bagman because Steve and his ilk would deliver product, thrust out a bag, and collect the money. Being a bagman may have seemed glamorous at the time, as Steve reckoned himself dashing; in fact, he still does. Truth be told, today a better use of the bag might be to place it over Steve's head as an act of mercy.

Now, Steve could go on for hours with stories about

eluding or escaping from "revenuers" or seedy competitors, but here are two choice tales which demonstrate that, next to Captain America, no one can stop or foil ol' Steve.

You may not realize it, but these bootleggers weren't dumb knuckleheads. They had it all figured out. No matter what scenario might unfold, they trained to execute the most effective response for each predicament.

So it was that one night, the law was hot on Steve's tail. This was not easy for the law, because Steve was not driving some *Beverly Hillbillies* jalopy. No siree. His vee-hick-ul was a souped-up muscle car. This time, though, Steve got himself into a real pickle. With the PO-lice nipping at his BE-hind, Steve came to a crick. This was no dilemma for Steve, for he had been well instructed—blow up that dang car and destroy the evidence.

Just so happens Steve had some dynamite in the trunk. Faster than you can say "Jumpin' Jehoshaphat," Steve took some sticks, don't know how many, to blow up the car. Before it could explode, Steve had already skedaddled through the crick up the opposite bank and into the woods. Then, ka-BOOM! Talk about your great balls of fire! Steve's eyes get as big as saucers even today as he regales the tale.

Oh, but there's more. This is where Jeanette comes in.

Seems one fine southern night Steve and his eye candy, Jeanette, were cruising down the road when two hot cars began to harass him. Now, Steve doesn't like being harassed. No, indeedy. Steve much prefers to do the harassing. In fact there's nothing that pleases Steve more than harassing anything—man, woman, child or inanimate object . . . that is, except Jeanette. Steve quivers like the great and mighty Oz when the curtain is pulled back when Jeanette gives him that "don't you dare" look, and for good reason, as you'll now see.

As Steve tells this story, he speaks in hushed tones and his eyes narrow, like a dentist leaning in to give you a root canal. "What will happen next?" I pant. I'm completely hooked at this point. Is ol' Steve going to get his comeuppance?

Why, hell no! That's hogwash, and I'm saying that about a place where there actually was hogwash, which is something you wouldn't wish on your worst enemy. Just as you can't keep a good man down, you can't keep a bad man down when that bad man is Steve Watkins.

The natural response for any normal person in this situation would be evade the enemy, or to use the vernacular, "done get your ass out of there." But, if you haven't learned by now, Steve is not a normal person. You could rightly say he's an abnormal person. You see, Steve decided being outnumbered by hooligans armed with powerful cars was a delightful situation because he was going to give them a big can of whup-ass.

At this point in the story, the two cars were in front of Steve hoping to cut him off. So, Steve does what any abnormal person would do—he put the pedal to the metal and floors it. Jeanette, terrified, could not bear to look. She ducked down and put her head in her lap. That car—like its frequent cargo—was pure white lightning. At some point, having perceived the inevitable collision had been averted, Jeanette popped up like Punxsutawney Phil—not to see her own shadow but to see the bad guys disappearing in theirs.

We could go on and on with this, but I will spare you. The real hero of *The Steve Watkins Story* is Jeanette. Her love for Steve is of biblical proportions. To believe that anyone could pass over the sins of Steve, nearly get killed by him, marry him, and stay married for sixty-two years is true faith, sho-nuff.

The moral to this story is simple but profound: Even a blind squirrel like Steve finds an acorn once in a while.

V
Assorted Morsels

Sandra Feen and Cliff Treyens

Benevolence of Servers
[Sandra]

To enter Tee Jaye's is to know we are expected.
We, in turn, can anticipate no problem
if we maneuver the same round table and awkward,
bulky chairs to accommodate canes, walkers, Wilma's
occasional stuffed animals, or a wheelchair, or cupcakes
and gag gifts for someone's birthday celebration,
since servers' benevolence brightens and elevates
a multitude of disruption, delight, or melancholy.
This, our syncopated rhythm: Brandy, Summer,
Holly, Stephanie, Brittany, Tina, Meghan,
and others, learning seasons of our faces.
They pour coffee through humor and gloom of
our narratives. We enter. They see us
dwindling, weather our deepening grief.
We still come, sometimes
sporadically. A holy steadiness,
strength in the familiar,
resolute, like
prayer.

Sandra Feen and Cliff Treyens

An American Woman's Montage
[Sandra]

Jeanette takes her first job,
first dinner order, at thirteen
at the Overlook Truck Stop
in Raccoon, Pennsylvania,
learning early the value
of studying others,
as well as behaving,
listening in school.
Women of her merit
are wanted in any work.

In Waco and Fort Worth,
she proves she can collect
gold stars for any training.
On land, forklift school,
and air, she parachutes
for Civil Air Patrol.
This is an interest and skill
she passes on years later
to daughters Anita and Amy,
and when Air Force calls,
she gives aid
during Xenia's '74 tornado.

But back in 1959,
her toughest job of the heart
comes at One Hour Valet,
Winston-Salem's dry cleaner.
She informs a customer named Steve
his shirts were thrown away
and takes his outrage.
He's quick to surmise
the last gal he fancied

responsible for his garments'
tragic demise at this
suitably-named dry cleaner,
her swift-scissor retaliation for
his blunt courtship end.

He's soaked in panic,
a salesman always on the go,
ready to make another
fresh-pressed presentation,
craving starched collars.
Jeanette tackled this tall,
cantankerous ex-football star
from day one,
without a button of training.
She foraged way back
in the dank mausoleum
of forgotten shirts. As if
it were dry cleaning kismet
and gender reversal,
Jeanette was Steve's Princess Savior
and Steve, Male Cinderella.
Yes. All shirts fit,
and this began their sixty years,
weaving them

into a married life
spent mostly in Columbus,
where she first cashiered
at the old Fort Hayes Hotel,
then became area manager
for *The Columbus Dispatch*,
driving the company truck through
dawn's nearly desolate streets.
For over fifty years,

There's a Rock on Martin Avenue

she bagged newspaper ads,
stitched steady, reliable income.
.
Now retired, she fastens effort
into a tale her grandkids direct.
They text and request orders
for ceramic Christmas trees of her design;
at the same time, her breakfast table buddies
at Tee Jaye's check out her newest
charm bracelet bling. Steve brags
about Jeanette's outdoor holiday wreaths,
while Jeanette's working on solving
a problem for a pal at the table.
At some point she'll tell Steve to
zip it up and listen.
Later, she shares a great joke
she'll need to repeat, since
Sandy is slow to understand.

Sandra Feen and Cliff Treyens

Ash Monday
[Sandra]

Cigar butt rests in a three-inch clear glass shoe
on a miniature knickknack shelf:
birthday party residue. Sixty-year-old female
grants earlier request to smoke
cigar with centenarian.
Nothing in her life commemorates sense
so deliciously
until this moment.

Sandra Feen and Cliff Treyens

No Other Response Needed
[Sandra]

"Take me as I is 'cause
I ain't changin'," Steve announces.

"All right, *Rosemary's Baby*," Ray says,
then lifts his empty coffee cup, looks
to meet the eyes of our waitress.

Sandra Feen and Cliff Treyens

Parade Day
[Cliff]

Everyone loves a parade. It's a spectacle to be sure, but one that unfolds *slowly*. The spectators trickle into Tee Jaye's Country Place. The regulars choose their spots and settle in with anticipation for what is to come, ordering their concessions.

Meanwhile, the parade vehicles *slowly* assemble in the parking lot—gleaming steel floats of vibrant colors. *Slowly, slowly,* the celebrities mount their floats, preparing to put on their game faces and to float-wave.

Like a rodeo clown, Steve warms up the crowd by sitting in his chair with his red-and-black **checked** suit; it's a signal that the parade is a'coming. He does not make too much a show of it as he is not the main attraction.

As the crowd inside builds, the parade is *slowly* making its way toward the entrance to the parade route, that is, the front door to Tee Jaye's. Ray's purple float, his rollator, is at the vanguard. As he *slowly* shuffles forward, the doors magically open as spectators clear the way for his entrance. Ray's is not a showy float. No, his is a modest float, one might say an "old school" float. What it lacks in flare it makes up in dependability. Let's just say Ray's float gets the job done and the crowd shows its appreciation with smiles, nods, and looks of admiration.

If Ray were to adorn his float with flowers, which he does not, it would be either red poppies—the kind they sell on Veterans Day—or yellow roses, the kind his beloved wife Jean liked when she was still in the parade with him.

The next float to arrive is Vern's, a sporty burgundy number that moves *slowly* along the circuitous parade route which snakes its way through the tables at Tee Jaye's. Vern's entrance is reminiscent of Roy Rogers upon his horse Trigger in the Rose Parade. Vern, atop his steed, so to speak, beams from ear to ear, head turning *slowly* side to side so as to please all the crowd, and right hand aloft *slowly* turning side to side at the wrist in that classic parade wave. It's a real crowd-pleaser that delights spectators.

If Vern were to adorn his float with flowers, it would be chamomiles, to reflect his calm demeanor and soothing presence.

Now, as everyone knows, in-between floats you need some walking dignitaries and, by golly, we got 'em. Bob walks in, adorned with flight jacket, aviator glasses, and his jet squadron cap, looking a bit like John Wayne in the movie *Flying Leathernecks.* Bob's irregular gait is reminiscent of the Duke's, and it is particularly pleasing to the ladies, which pleases Bob immensely.

If a flyboy like Bob could adorn himself with flowers, it might be tulips—well designed and aerodynamic.

Last but certainly not least is Wilma and her gleaming aqua rollator float. Wilma is the parade queen, standing atop her carriage, grandly smiling and relishing every moment. No one enjoys being in a parade more than Wilma, who cannot help but smile, wave, apply lipstick, and toss occasional witticisms to the spectators. Her **blonde** hair and colorful parade attire truly befit a parade queen. The only thing missing is the sash.

If Wilma could adorn her float with flowers, it would be

black-eyed Susans to represent the black eyes she sustained from a fall one time. Only Wilma could march in a parade with two black eyes and love every minute of it.

Why do people love parades so much? I have a hunch. As a parade attendant, I have a unique perspective to observe both the parade and the crowd.

The people on parade floats are special. They are there for a reason. They're admired. People *in* the parade are often lovely, accomplished, distinguished, recognized, and, frankly, have lived enough life to be on a float.

So it is with the Tee Jaye's parade. From my vantage point, the parade watchers are clearly delighted at what they see. I sense they look up to Ray, 100; Vern, ninety; Bob, ninety-three; and Wilma, ninety-one; they are of the "Greatest Generation."

The minute the parade begins the place lights up. Doors fly open. Our Dominican waitress Stephanie shouts a hello and waves; onlookers smile and turn their heads; and, like Mardi Gras parade spectators groveling for beads, some patrons can barely stay in their **seats but for to talk** with one of the float personalities.

How appropriate that patron spectators at Tee Jaye's find something worthy in people like them who have attained parade status. Like a friendly neighborhood bar where people parade in and out, there's a predictability and familiarity about the whole scene that does the heart good.

Sandra Feen and Cliff Treyens

VI
Come What May

Sandra Feen and Cliff Treyens

A Broken Record
[Cliff]

In the Gospel of Matthew, the disciple Peter, who always seemed to be sticking his foot in his mouth, asks Jesus, "Lord, how often shall my brother sin against me and I forgive him? Up to seven times?"

You can almost hear Peter's exasperation at one of the other disciples, maybe that darn John or James or maybe even the sleazy former tax-gatherer Matthew, in which case Matthew gets the last laugh by recording Peter's vexation in perpetuity.

"I do not say to you, up to seven times, but up to seventy times seven," Jesus responds. Let me see . . . that's 490 times to be exact. In other words, Peter should forgive as many times as he has cause to forgive. I guess it takes the power of God to love like Jesus.

"Jesus Christ! How long to I have to put up with this?" we say. That's what some of my friends remark at my incessantly repeated "dad jokes." Like this one—

"I just got diagnosed with Dunlop's disease," I say with a solemn face.

"Oh, no! What is it," my acquaintance asks with a mix of perplexity and concern.

"It's where your belly done lops over your belt," I reply. Groans and laughs inevitably follow, but my wife, Cathy, who has heard this joke literally hundreds of times is not amused.

Worse yet is hearing something over and over and over

in a single encounter. "Not again," we say in our heads. "How many times do I have to listen to this?"

Seventy times seven, I've come to learn. The love of Jesus is deep; one of those things that surpasses understanding.

When my mom Jean's dementia became pronounced, she would repeat questions or comments over and over, often multiple times within ten minutes or so. When this happened, I could feel the impatience and vexation welling up inside me; even anger at my inability to reason with someone incapable of reasoning.

At some point, I don't know why, it dawned on me that Mom was never going to change. That's not exactly a revelation, but it seemed so to me. I came to realize that the only way I could relate to her was to be interested in what she had to say every time she said it, even if it was 490 times.

The epiphany—this wasn't about me. It was about loving her. To listen to her say or ask the same thing over and over and over again wasn't something to endure. It was a way to love my mom whose memory was fading.

The weekend before she died in an accidental fall, my new-found patience led to one of the sweetest moments of my life. I arrived at her memory care facility to pick her up for lunch at my house. She was sitting in the central common area.

"Do you want to come to my house for lunch?" I asked.

"Who are you?" she said.

There's a Rock on Martin Avenue

"I'm Cliff, your son," I replied.

Surprised and most pleased by this news, she turned to the other dementia and Alzheimer's patients, waved her hand through the air with a flourish and declared, "This is my son!" To this the other residents applauded with shouts of "Yay!"

I'll never forget that moment . . . until I do.

Later I would have ample opportunity to practice this kind of love around the Wednesday breakfast table each week at Tee Jaye's Country Place with Vern, God rest his soul. A former middle school and high school history teacher, Vern probably forgot more history that I ever knew in the first place. But there were some things he remembered, and we got to hear those some things over and over at the breakfast table each week.

He loved to tell of a historic rock on Martin Avenue in the Bottoms on the west side of Columbus, Ohio, near where he grew up. We heard about it so many times that Vern inadvertently gave us the title to this book.

Every time Vern mentioned the rock on Martin Avenue, I'd say excitedly, "I've seen that rock. In fact, I visited the rock because of you!" This never failed to delight ol' Vern. He pretty much had a big smile on his face the whole time we were at Tee Jaye's, and I'm talking two hours-plus.

Another of his favorite factoids which he liked to share is this—

"I . . . I . . . ah . . . I grew up on Meek Avenue," he'd say with a sly smile. For some mysterious reason, Vern remembered this dialogue he and I shared. Like a pitcher's wind-up, Vern's opening statement was nothing more than a thinly veiled setup for my punch line.

"Vern, I find that very i . . . ron . . . ic," I responded slowly, with emphasis. At this, Vern's mouth opened in a state of suspension and his eyes widened waiting for the rest.

"You should have been born on Outrageous Street or Audacious Boulevard," I say semi-sarcastically. To this, Vern chortled, his smile widened and his eyes crinkled.

Then frequently less than a minute later he'd say the same thing, and we'd do it again, often three or four times. It never got old. We were enjoying one another, like dancing. I was just following Vern's lead. That gave Vern dignity and both of us joy.

Jesus had it right. That knucklehead Peter (you could substitute "we") wanted to get past this forgiveness thing and have the self-satisfaction of not forgiving. But Jesus loved Peter too much to give him what he wanted. Jesus met him at his point of need; that is, the need to learn patience, forgiveness, and ultimately how to love.

Vern isn't the only one at the breakfast table who struggles with poor memory. None of us are getting any younger. Just this morning I went on a walk with someone and part of the way in realized I forgot to put on my glasses. Multiple times a week I purposefully walk into a room only to wonder why I'm there.

I sure miss Vern and talking about the rock on Martin Avenue, Meek Avenue, circus elephants marching down Mound Street, delivering papers to Pappy's Pool Hall, and dozens of other memory snippets I've heard a hundred times. Like a broken record that's keeps repeating, those stories were music to my ears. I just want to keep dancing to the tune.

Sandra Feen and Cliff Treyens

Falling
[Cliff]

I don't remember the first time my elderly parents started falling. But like vivid scenes in a movie, some of my parents' falls are indelibly etched on my mind.

There are many things about aging parents, or aging for that matter, that sneak up on you. It shouldn't be a surprise, but somehow it is. Falling is one of those things. It seems one day your folks are happily going about enjoying their mobility, and then they start falling.

There is nothing that makes one feel more helpless and terrified than watching an elderly parent fall. My experience is that for every fall I've witnessed, there are many more I haven't—and I don't think I'm alone in this.

I'll never forget the call I received on May 29, 2017, at about 6:30 AM.

"I just got a call. Mom has had a fall," said Dad, his voice shaking.

Then five minutes later he called again, "She's dead."

Just that fast, Mom, who I'd picked up from her memory care unit two days before for lunch at my house, was gone. Mercifully she died instantly and was spared a long, slow demise. Little did I know that soon I would be on high alert for my falling dad.

Mom was only in memory care for one month. But the many months Dad labored as her sole caregiver had weakened him considerably. When I'd visit him at home after her death, there'd be signs that Dad, too, was falling.

Smears of blood would be on the screen door and about the house. Dad would be showing "senile purpura," those benign purple blotches that appear beneath the papery skin of older adults. This occurs when the skin and the blood vessels become more fragile as one ages, making it easier for the skin to bruise from minor trauma. At sixty-eight, I'm getting them now. Of course, the not-so-minor trauma leaves even more gnarly bruises.

Then Dad's grocery list began to include Band-Aids, and I don't mean just the regular, assorted sizes. I mean big ones, more like patches—the kind you can put over bleeding elbows. For more than a year, Dad's elbows were perpetually scabbed from repeated backward falls.

Many elderly people fall forward or in place, or so Google tells me. But Dad always fell backward, which can be symptomatic of something called "posture instability." Dad walked bent over at nearly a 45-degree angle when using his walker.

It took about a year after Mom's death to get much of his strength back, but it was during this time that I started to go on high alert whenever I was around Dad. I still think sadly of the time he and I were preparing to go to a Minor League Baseball game. As I went to pull the car up, I asked him to stay seated so I could help him get into the car. As soon as I turned my back, I heard him say, "Whoa . . . ." He had stood up and, that quick, he fell back, banging his head against a brick wall, blood pouring down the back of his head.

I rushed him to an urgent care, not wanting to initiate a six-hour wait in an emergency room. Probably not a good

There's a Rock on Martin Avenue

decision because of the possible concussion risk.

But Dad was an exceptional human being in many ways, and being a centenarian was just one. His hard head was another. I've known multiple people who have fallen once and suffered serious, lasting concussion trauma. Yet Dad repeatedly bounced his head on brick and concrete, and except for some blood loss seemed none the worse for it.

One particularly gruesome fall occurred the day I decided to replace his useless screen door with a new one. This was a typical home repair job for me; a two-hour task turned into a six-hour task. At one point, weary and frustrated from my ineptitude, I turn my head to see Dad standing on the three-foot-high concrete stoop.

Why these falls seem to happen in slow motion, I don't know. As I watched, Dad began to fall backward; I screamed, then he hit the deck and his head bounced with a thud off the concrete. Surely this would be a hospital visit, but no. Even though he had another gusher on the back of his noggin, I was able to help Dad to his feet, bandage his head and elbows, and as far as I could tell, he was otherwise okay. Miraculously, there were no lasting effects.

Not all his falls left him unscarred. Once, Dad, a master of understatement, ignored his infected finger until it was three times the size the others, and the docs had to amputate half of it.

The finger incident led to another, life-altering fall. Before Dad was hospitalized for the finger, he was so weakened by the infection that he fell at home and couldn't get up. I tried calling him on a Sunday night to get an update on the finger. There was no answer, and I assumed he went to bed early to rest up.

The next morning, after calling repeatedly and getting no answer, I hightailed it over to his house. Upon unlocking the side door, I heard him bark, "Come back here." I go to his bedroom and there he is, sprawled on the floor having been there all night—dehydrated, bruised, and weary.

"I decided something," he said resolutely, looking up from the floor.

"What?" I asked.

"I'm going to stop driving," he said.

"That's good," I replied. "Do you think it's time to go to assisted living?" I asked.

"Yes," he said.

And just like that, this fall persuaded Dad to do two things I'd been urging him to do ever since Mom died. I won't say that the fall was worth it, as that would cruel, but it reminded me of one of my favorite Bible verses, Romans 8:28, "We know that God causes everything to work together for the good of those who love God and are called according to His purpose." In this instance, all I could say to that was a big "Amen!"

As for the other Breakfast Club members, they've all fallen. Bob and Vern have both fallen at Tee Jaye's. I'm certain Steve has fallen though he probably wouldn't admit it if had. And Wilma, boy, oh boy, did she have a doozy.

One day Wilma shows up to breakfast and it looked as though someone had hit her in the face with a blueberry pie. Her entire face was different patterns and hues of purple. To top it off, she had two black eyes. I wouldn't have believed it if I hadn't seen for myself. My reaction was similar to when I laid eyes on Dad's bloated finger. I could barely keep from barfing. Let me just say, being around people who fall is not for the faint-hearted.

Wilma, on the other hand, seemed quite unperturbed or self-conscious. Just as usual, she was wisecracking, making racy comments and complaining about the food. It was reassuring to see that she was okay—a tough old bird, just like Dad.

I've had many falls during my forty-plus-years' running career, which ended several years ago due to meniscus problems in both knees. Those falls weren't from old age but from running in the dark and on uneven sidewalks. Then, I was exceptionally sure-footed. Why, one time I was competing in a sixty-mile trail run near the Cumberland Gap in Tennessee. Upon scampering up a steep climb, an observer exclaimed, "That guy is like a goat!" No kidding.

Nearly thirty years later, my considerably weaker legs and diminishing balance have conspired to cause falls on a number of occasions with hardly any provocation or consequences. One of the more humorous incidences occurred when I got tangled up in my own feet and ingloriously tumbled on the bedroom carpet. Both my wife, Cathy, and I got a good guffaw out of that one.

However, I see the handwriting on the wall. It won't be long before the son becomes like the father. So, I have started using an elliptical machine at a gym and praying I will use a cane, walker, or wheelchair sooner rather than later so as not to unnecessarily worry my loved ones.

Dad always minimized his propensity to fall until shortly before his death. In answer to the nurse doing his assessment for admission to hospice, Dad overstated things in saying falling was his biggest problem. Then confined to bed, Dad never fell again. Within a week he was dead.

For all of us who make it to old age, I suppose some amount of falling is as inevitable as gravity.

When it's all said and done, as trying as it can be, the trauma and heartache of falling loved ones is far outweighed by the privilege of being there for them. Solomon had it right when he wrote Ecclesiastes 4:9–10.

"Two are better than one because they have a good return for their labor. For if either of them falls, the one will lift up his companion. But woe to the one who falls when there is not another to lift him up."

To that, I say, "Amen."

Hospicetality
[Cliff]

Hospice. There are many words I've associated with it—dread, fear, cancer, terminal, and death, to name a few; but a word that never entered my mind was beautiful.

Isn't it strange how one can have such strong notions about something foreign to you? The mention of hospice reliably conjured up visions of silent, grim nurses, IVs, medicinal smells, and unresponsive people in hospital beds waiting to die.

Yet it took only a few of days for my conceptions to be shattered as I watched my dad's (Ray) remarkable death in the care of hospice. I swear, the people I saw tending to him were not silent, grim nurses at all. They were angels.

His decline came quickly. Based on the recommendation of his assisted living facility, Dad was evaluated and approved for hospice. Ten days later he went on around-the-clock hospice care. Three days after that, Dad died.

In those final three days, except for one night's sleep, I was there around-the-clock with the nurses—a total of five different ones during hospice care. How could these nurses go about their business without being perpetually depressed? They are in the midst of death daily. Even so, I witnessed people who not only were diligent in their tenderness, but honored to step in the gap between life and death to provide comfort when it mattered the most to the patient and the family, or more pointedly, to me.

I learned that angels don't have to be of the angelic realm. They're regular people earning a living even as they tend to the dying. One was a mother of young children, another the mom of young adults. Then there was the young lady right out of nursing school who'd been married only a few years.

I was touched by the veteran nurse who had a son in the Army. She lingered over a photo on the wall of Dad and his B-24 crew crewmates walking toward the camera. They'd just completed a bombing mission over Europe in World War II. She couldn't wait to tell her soldier son about it. Dad, a man she didn't know, was without a doubt a hero, she said. And from her he received care deserving of a hero.

What was taking place in that efficiency apartment was not about *me*, but every one of the nurses was pleased to talk with me. We had conversations about all kinds of things such as family, interests, what gets us up in the morning, and God, to name a few. No matter that we were strangers. Brought together for a common purpose, we engaged in what we relational humans were made to do so well. We talked.

I was struck, too, by how attentive the nurses were to explaining everything they did for Dad—and not just to me, but to Dad.

When a nurse saw Dad shifting uncomfortably, for instance, she explained that she would place pillows strategically so as to provide support where it was needed. When his feet were cold to the touch, the nurse told Dad she was going to cover them.

They talked to Dad just as if he was sitting up and paying attention even though he was on his back and noncommunicative. "Hearing is the last thing to go," every nurse said. So, occasionally, I'd get right in his ear and tell him I loved him. I also reminded Dad, "Mom is waiting for you in Heaven, and I'll be coming soon."

On numerous occasions, they'd change Dad. In consideration of his dignity, I chose to leave the room at those times. However, near the end, I witnessed a poignant moment that I'll treasure.

About one hour before he died, a young nurse said, "Mr. Ray, I'm going to turn you on your side and make you nice and clean." Then she slowly and gently pushed him onto his side and took a damp cloth and cleaned him—as gently and lovingly as if he were her baby. Then she patted him dry and gently lowered him to his back. "Mr. Ray, I'm done," she said, neatly tucking the sheets around him.

My heart was moved to see this act of care and kindness. It made no difference to her that he would die very soon. Like each of the nurses who preceded her, she was not just taking care of Dad, she was devoted to him just as if she had known him all her life.

There has been much criticism of the medical community's shortcomings when it comes to patient care. There was even a movie about it called *The Doctor*. Actor William Hurt played a brusque doctor whose perfunctory and sometimes rude behavior left patients and families emotionally wounded—that is, until he got diagnosed with cancer. Being on the receiving end of medical care forever changed him. He beat cancer. Then, like the nurses who were watching over Dad, Hurt's character morphed into an empathetic doctor who showed tender loving care for his patients.

I could not have asked for anything more. Dad died peacefully and comfortably, less than two months from turning 101. There was little I could do in those last days other than be there. Yet, I am comforted to know that Dad has by now met Jesus, is reunited with Mom, and will be there with open arms when I join him someday.

Furthermore, I am comforted beyond words to know that five angels were blessing Dad with the best of care to the very end. It was beautiful.

Letting Go
[Cliff]

In America, there is a coming of age for many teenagers that few other moments match. It's that day when a set of car keys is handed over to you. Then there's the thrilling moment when it's just you, sitting in the car, ready to go out there, somewhere to a place of your choosing. It is a freedom and independence like no other.

I remember it well. My Great-aunt Kay passed along her 1961 Ford Falcon to my brother. When he had run the crap out of it, the old bird was passed along to me. I didn't care that it chugged rather than hummed, or that when it rained the car tended to stall out. Even the manual choke was of no concern to me.

I had a car, and if I wanted to go somewhere in it, I could. Ah, freedom!

To use driving terminology, now put it in reverse. Imagine rather than receiving your first set of keys, you're handing over your last set of keys . . . for good. In our culture of independence, this can be a wrenching experience to an older person. It's as though your world has suddenly shrunk, leading to a sort of imprisonment.

I know, not because I've had to do so, but because I was in the unenviable position of trying to convince my dad, Ray, to do so. It is a process, and I do mean process, we children of the Breakfast Club members have had to initiate with much trepidation. When it's time to begin that process, the elderly parent's gut is not the only one being wrenched.

For years, after Dad turned ninety, I asked him whether it

was time to give up driving.

"I'm fine!" he said dismissively. Those two words and the way he said them clearly communicated that this conversation was off limits.

Knowing how my own flexibility, reaction time, and tendency to drift left or right of my lane was increasing, I would periodically bring it up.

"Dad, do you think it's time to give up driving?" I'd ask again.

"I'm fine!" he'd say gruffly.

Dad didn't see irony in the fact that years before he'd been pulled over by a police officer who thought he was drunk because of his weaving. Dad was stone sober, but his driving was impaired. Some artificial intelligence entity explained it to me this way—

"Age-related declines in vision, slower reaction times, reduced physical dexterity, and cognitive changes, which can make it difficult to maintain a steady course often cause (the elderly) to unintentionally drift across lane lines without realizing it."

Yikes! The entity may be artificial, but the intelligence is spot on. Why, I'm only about to turn seventy, and already my wife will not let me adjust anything on the dashboard while driving. If I take my eyes off the road for even a millisecond I drift right or left.

At one point, I considered invoking my right under state law to require Dad to take a driving test. I remember a wise friend who had gone through this experience. He reasoned that to demand such a test when one knows it is necessary for a loved one's welfare and the safety of others was the only responsible thing to do.

I thought about it, by God, and I came to the conclusion that he was right! Then I . . . chickened out. I just couldn't muster the courage to do what was in everyone's best interests.

It took a night on the floor after falling to convince Dad—or more accurately, for him to admit—that he no longer was in good enough physical shape to be driving. Color me shocked (*not*) that when cleaning out Dad's house, I found a letter from his auto insurance carrier dropping his coverage due to multiple minor accidents, forcing him to pay exorbitant rates for another insurer.

Likewise, our breakfast buddy, Wilma, also did not let go easily. There were signs something was amiss with her driving. Bob noticed after one breakfast that her sporty red car had a ding on the right side. He was quite interested in how that ding got there but as far as I know, he never got to the bottom of it. We all had our suspicions regarding Wilma's driving.

The straw that broke the camel's back was the day she let her car roll into her closed garage door. While the car was not damaged much, the door was totaled.

Even after Wilma's keys were confiscated, she could never be confined. When she moved into assisted living, Wilma quickly became a flight risk and a bit of a Houdini, discovering how to break out of her lockdown memory care unit in ways that baffled the management. She even conspired to break out with Vern, who was in the same memory care unit. Like Butch Cassidy and the

Sundance Kid, they made a slippery escape, only to be caught at a nearby store, licking their chops, having satiated themselves like two delinquent kids with a bag of candy.

Bob, ninety-four, is still driving at this writing. His trusty and slightly rusty minivan with the license plate "Sr Pilot" can still be found in the Tee Jaye's Country Place parking lot when the few Breakfast Club members left still convene.

A former jet fighter pilot, Bob occasionally gets into the "cockpit" of his vintage motor coach, which he has used to take long trips north, south, east, and west of Ohio. I suppose as a concession to age, Bob rarely uses it anymore. He has not, however, let go of it. Bob managed to finagle a parking spot at a secure military installation, and every once in a while, he goes over there and runs it to circulate the engine fluids and prevent his gaskets from drying out.

I jokingly goaded Bob and the gang to take a cross country trip in the motor coach. Imagine it— Bob behind the wheel with his aviator sunglasses piloting the ship and talking to no one in particular; Steve and Vern at a table in the middle bickering about some inconsequential thing, while Wilma chortles and zaps both of them with one-liners that would make Don Rickles blush; and my Dad sitting in the back with a newspaper and cup of coffee alternately sipping and snoozing, seemingly oblivious to the road show.

Surprisingly, Vern, ever the contrarian, let go of the car keys relatively easily. One of his last solo drives was to buy multiple copies of the local newspaper with his latest editorial submission. With that accomplished and his dementia accelerating, Vern pretty much lost interest in driving.

If there is anyone in the Feen family who should give up the keys, it may be his daughter and coauthor of this book, Sandy. Out of her own mouth comes the following, almost-unbelievable true story.

Not all that long ago, Sandy had arrived at some destination parking lot to pull into a parking space. This was not parallel parking, mind you, but one of those straight-ahead parking spots with two widely separated lines. Easy-peasy, right?

Well, Sandy didn't cut the wheels quite right and lopped over one of the lines. She reversed the car, tried to straighten the wheel and took another crack at it. This time the car was cockeyed in the other direction. You know how a large semi-truck wiggles side to side and goes back and forth blocking the road while trying to go reverse up to a loading dock? Sandy's maneuvering was something like that but she was always one bubble shy of plumb.

She also resembled a driver bombed after too many drinks who's seeing four lines instead of two and not able to get straight between any of them. In fact, an observer, convinced that this was precisely the case, called the police to stop Sandy before someone or something got hurt.

Upon arrival, the police officer could see that clearly the lady behind the wheel was toasted. But, of course, to prosecute the case, law enforcement would need evidence—so the officer ordered Sandy to take a breathalyzer test. Sandy, quite flustered at this point—

and in her flustration sounding very much like a boozer—explained that, in fact, she was quite sober (that's what they all say). But the officer would have none of it, and the breathalyzer was administered.

Imagine the officer's surprise at discovering Sandy was, in fact, sober. Stone sober. To this day it remains a mystery to everyone why she could not pull the car properly into that parking space.

As for me, the question is not will I give up the keys but how. I've already proclaimed that I will voluntarily give up my keys no later than age eighty-five, if I live that long. You would think that's laudatory, but every time I mention it, people either blow it off as bluster, or they try to talk me out of it for some reason.

More likely than not, I'll simply get tired of losing my car keys. I've lost a set of car keys twice recently and just ordered a back-up key in anticipation of the next time. Perhaps as a benefit to society God will intervene once again, and the third time will be a charm.

Pill Popping and Dropping
[Cliff]

Taking pills is an indispensable part of old age in America. Why, I'm less than one year shy of seventy and I have two pill organizers already—one for everyday use and one for trips.

But my real education in the perils and foibles of pill taking was in watching Dad (Ray) take, or rather try to gobble down, his pills. Over the nearly seven years of weekly breakfasts with him, I've learned that pill popping and pill dropping are another manifestation of failing eyesight, uncooperative hands, and poor pill-taking technology.

At first, I thought "How hard can it be to take pills?" Today, I think "Why is it so hard to take pills?"

When I first started my weekly breakfasts with Dad, he'd bring his few pills in an empty pill container. Once he got the pill container out of his pocket, he'd simply remove the lid and take them. But before long, Dad getting his big hand in and out of his pants pocket became quite an ordeal. At times, it could take five minutes before he could pull it off.

Then I came up with the brilliant idea of putting the pill container in a baggie, which he would place in the seat of his rollator. This worked for a while, but then his clumsy hands—hampered by numbness in his fingers—made it difficult to open the baggie. Next, I got him a fanny pack which never rested on his fanny but which he instead kept in the rollator seat. I got the fanny pack with the biggest, easiest zipper. That seemed to work okay until he died.

But there were other obstacles to pills getting from the container into his mouth. When Dad would dump those pills in his hand, a number of things could happen. He might pour them into his palm, but one or more might roll onto the floor. Or, as he moved his hand to his mouth, gravity would grab hold of a pill or two down to the floor. Other times, some of the pills would go in his mouth and others would stick to his palm and end up on the floor.

The two most suspenseful events at breakfast were Dad taking his pills and his trips to the men's room. Both took a long time. While he regularly dropped pills, fortunately, he never fell on his men's room trips, although he did fall regularly in his assisted living unit.

I've often wondered, why isn't there a way for old people to take pills without all these problems? So, I researched this on the web. I was surprised to learn that apparently no one on the planet Earth has yet to figure it out. One website had this lame idea—

"Fill a plastic water or soda bottle with water. Put the tablet on your tongue and close your lips tightly around the bottle opening. Take a drink, keeping contact between the bottle and your lips and using a sucking motion to swallow the water and pill. Don't let air get into the bottle."

Good grief! Why, getting a tiny pill on an old person's tongue can be tantamount to walking on a tightrope over Niagara Falls. Filling a soda bottle with water? Fat chance. Coordinating lips and sucking at the same time—horsefeathers! There's a reason why they charge you for dispensing pills at assisted living—it's the only way to make sure the pills end up in the resident's stomachs.

I figured another thing out with Dad. One reason old people's prescriptions run out so quickly is because half the pills end up on the floor. When Dad died and I was cleaning out his room, I found dozens of pills all over the place—under the bed, behind furniture, strewn about in cabinets. And that's not all.

I also found Atomic FireBalls everywhere. You see, Dad developed a hankering for Atomic FireBall candy at Tee Jaye's Country Place, where they sold them at the register. When Tee Jaye's exhausted its supply, I searched all over town but couldn't find more. So, I ordered a bin of 225 Atomic FireBalls online, which lasted him to the end of his life with a bunch to spare in the bin and on the floor.

Another problem with pills is that it's more difficult than you might imagine for one to remember if you took pills for a given day. This is why daily, weekly, and monthly pill dispensers were invented. The problem is that the daily assortment of pills must be placed in those little daily compartments. And, remembering what day it is— or whether or not one has taken the day's pills—is not as easy as it might seem. Believe me, I speak from personal experience.

Not too long before Dad died, I got him a weekly pill dispenser that had Monday through Sunday for both AM and PM, since some of his pills were taken in the morning and others right before bedtime. To ensure success, I filled the little compartments myself. After only a week, I discovered that Dad took his pills most but not all of the days.

Regardless, Dad nearly lived to 101, and I miss him with fond affection. When I was cleaning out his room, the strewn pills, Atomic FireBalls, stale cookies, the ouzo shot glass I gave him, and other reminders on the floor made me a bit melancholy.

The writing is on the wall for me. Even before I retired, I got my first inkling of what awaited me one day as I stood next to a coworker at the men's room urinals. We're standing there for what seemed minutes. Then the sound of drop after drop from the two of us as if in stereo while we stared straight at the wall ten inches from our faces waiting for more to happen. Eventually, this turned into two trickles as if the facets were not entirely off.

"Where's the Flomax when you need it," my coworker deadpanned. I roared with laughter.

I'm not laughing now. Flomax is the first prescription drug I started taking. Sad to say, but I recommended it to Dad, who also got on it. Even with the drug, it's not like it used to be. I once peed "like a Canadian racehorse" as a friend used to say. Now I pee like a geriatric Mr. Ed. And get this—more than once I've discovered that when my flow is not at the max, I forgot, you heard it, I forgot to take my Flomax.

I'm now up to three prescription drugs and four over-the-counter allergy meds and vitamins a day. It's true what they say—the acorn doesn't fall far from the tree. And so the legacy continues.

VII
The End of an Era

Sandra Feen and Cliff Treyens

There's a Rock on Martin Avenue

Vern and Wilma's Last Tee Jaye's Sunday Together
[Sandra]

Everything was harder, last October Sunday—
Lori and I maneuvered our parents
out of memory care, drove them from Grove City
to the east side of Columbus for our two-hour ritual
    breakfast,
like dozens and dozens of Sundays.
We waited longer than normal for the nurse

on duty to dispense Dad's meds, found that she was new
and untrained. I tried to retrieve his meds myself, since
he was already falling deeper into sleep in his chair.
Wilma was distraught over something missing in her
    walker seat,
but unsure what it was. As soon as Dad was awake,
we made certain he remembered to swallow, helped him
    stand,
noticed he was beltless, which meant aides forgot to put
    it on.
Even with one in place, we always grip the back of his
    pants
to insure balance.

Lori gave me the look that meant I could run to his room
to get it while she stayed with him. I did,
and we threaded it through the loops without Dad even
realizing and Lori began the trek, holding Dad's pants
because, of course, he preferred that she took the job of
    him,
while I caught up with Wilma, who was
already there—always the first at the coded security door,
so ready to move, always leading our way.

But resident Jerry snickered,

made fun of Dad needing assistance
and the fact that two of us put on his belt.
Lori motioned me to backtrack to him,
get a morsel of emotional satisfaction
in a place so void of it. I conjured one of my old teacher
facial expressions I used when I wanted to scold
a student for bullying, one of my pet peeves. You see,

some personality traits don't get lost,
even in a memory-care facility.
I stood in purposeful proximity to this resident bully
who yesterday tried to push his girlfriend out of her
    wheelchair
because he said he was tired of her,
and I was relieved I was in the right hallway
at the right time to wheel her to safety.
"What, honey?" he cocked his head back, like a turkey.
"Stop. Enough," and the glossy blue slime
of his eyes locked in clarity
with my flaming-bitch brown glare. No need to elaborate.
"All right. Back off, blondie," he said.

I flew to the door, coded us out, hastily locked
the door on other faces begging to leave with us.
We helped Dad into his wheelchair
that waited just on this side, so he had enough energy
    between
the exit and parking lot to my car. It took every muscle
of ingenuity to get him into his passenger seat.

We never pondered that day's audacity of change.
Lori and I opened all car doors, as if hoping a spiced
    miracle
would breeze in, attempting from all angles to steer,
    cajole, pull

ankles in. He was breathing, blinking,
but limbs were dead weight.
Sixty-year-old contortionists, we were upside down on
   his torso.
He was our jungle gym.

All the while, Wilma stood outside, waited without
   complaint.
She exuded first-time patience, not threatening to stomp
   down
to the railroad tracks, not directing Dad to move his ass,
not imploring me for lipstick or rolling her eyes at Lori.
Not hearing the percussive clatter of her enormous
   personality
filled me with fear. A heavy irritation, confusion.
And a metal rod of remorse.

I don't remember much else. I'm not sure how we got
   Dad
out of the car to our group at Tee Jaye's. I just remember
the eyes of our chosen family watching
as we came closer to the sanctuary of their collective
   silence,
tender gaze. Steve's eyes were excessively kind, and
   Donna's,
a soft warmth. A table of five in tentative wait;
it was the last time Wilma led the four of us in.

Then November wept into our lives,
the month Dad and Wilma both died.

Sandra Feen and Cliff Treyens

There's a Rock on Martin Avenue

Aside
[Sandra]

My dad, Vern, cherished a photo with Mom—and
   Wilma,
Bob, and Ray with their spouses—taken at a HomeTown
   Buffet
Valentine's dinner for couples married over fifty years.
He carried it in his walker until he lost it again and again,
but it came back to him. His daughters hunted it down
in all the right places, with his name in permanent
marker on the back of the frame.

Wilma also came to live at Ashford, had a copy of the
   photo
in her walker, too (until she didn't), when she wasn't
   piling
a dog-and-bear collection in her seat or stuffing it with
blouses and bras on a night she was trying to break out
   and
convince Vern to come. "I love ya, honey, but you're not
   clever
or fast enough on your own two feet.
Move your bloomin' butt," and when she really
meant business, demanded "Move your ass."
He'd utter a soft giggle, grip his handles tighter
as if he had fresh incentive to try

harder. One day his legs proved healthier, his mind
clear enough for a little rebellion.
I received a call that they were gone,
their whereabouts, unknown—for a few minutes,
   anyway.
They were found next door, buying candy at CVS—
had it all eaten before they were caught
and returned.

"Well, did either of you save me a piece?"
I said to two people who looked at me
as if I were scolding.
"You never told us to, honey," Wilma retorted.

When Dad could still speak he would pull me aside,
say with a stutter: "W-W-W-Wilmmma. I've-v-v-v gg got
something to to say. A-b-bout HER," his eyes a round,
unclouded declaration. "Sh–she's n-not w-with it, not with it.
I'm telling you—" then a knock at his door:

"Honey, come out here . . . ." Wilma pulled me into the hall.
"You need to know this. He's not playing with a full deck.
He's left his brain in that red cap of his, honey.
He's had too many naps, honey, and another thing . . . ."
and say it again. And again.

And again.
And they both shared their concern with conviction
that they were the best keeper and protector for the other,
kissing each other's hands at meal times and each day's end.

So when she died, I knew it wouldn't be long
before Dad followed her. It made comedic sense
Wilma went faster than he did.
Excruciating pain took him four days later.
Near his end, his eyes briefly

fluttered open.
I held up the HomeTown Buffet photo,
where Wilma sat next to Mom.

"They are sitting next to each other again, Dad,
and waiting for you," then I whispered
an aside I never thought would be my last words to him—
"So move your ass."

Sandra Feen and Cliff Treyens

Comforter
[Sandra]

"I'm sure this is such a hard time of change, grief, and loss for you. These last years have been so devoted to your dad that I imagine you almost don't know who you are now or how to begin again," writes childhood friend Ann—also daughter of John, one of the oldest members of the breakfast table, who used to pick up Dad, Vern, and Ray, when they could no longer drive.

John exuded quiet strength, in steady loyal service to his friends. He remained cognitively sharp attending Tee Jaye's into his nineties, until he no longer felt he could simultaneously navigate Ray's faster Sunday maneuvering in and out of the car, with Vern's slow brittle drag, along with Vern's annoying linger in the restaurant when everyone else was long ready to leave, both Sundays and Wednesdays.

Bob began picking up Ray on Sundays, while Cliff continued to drive his dad Ray on men's group Wednesdays. John handed over twice weekly driving reigns of Vern to me and to Jenny. He spooned calm, fatherly training over the phone, his soothing effort of preparing us for next layers of adventures with Dad, where the Wednesday men's group would baptize us into their midweek banter as their first female cohorts, until a year later Sunday's Wilma and Jeanette joined Hump Day hilarity.

All siblings, children's spouses, and other family members spirited the core group at some point. In my family, Jenny worked hard to keep Dad feeling independent. Early on, she waited for him in the parking lot so he could maintain space with his friends. Any pristinely creased pants and ironed shirt worn by Dad was Jenny's doing, continuing Mom's decades of care. Polly came to the table from North Carolina and played the piano for his memory care facility for a week. Holly traveled from Michigan and visited the table monthly, often there for birthday bashes. Pete served in my place if a poetry event took me out of town, and Cliff's brother Jim flew in from Washington State when Cliff and Cathy were traveling.

John and his effervescent Joan made only rare visits back to our table, and while we relished the rekindling heat of their friendship, John and Joan made a decisive shift to savor golden sheltering days of time at home, and when their next juncture came, it also arrived on their own terms. Interestingly, their assisted living transition coincided with Dad's final exit, in the uniquely cozy Cotner Funeral Home, where Dad's memorial was held.

They were there with Ann to show support to all of Vern's family, and to give gifts: a scrapbook of photos from earlier propitious breakfasts, along with a comforter, where roses lavished a bronze autumn background of quilted splashes of color, lovingly applicated.

"Enjoy your rest and your memories, while you can," John advised.

Sandra Feen and Cliff Treyens

How to Repurpose
[Sandra]

Wrap pine with charger cord.
Make it garland. Make each hearing aid
an ornament, with appropriate hint of traditional
Christmas color—left hearing aid, daub of green; right,
  red.
Red is right, red is right, chant it:
"Red is right and right is red,
just keep that one thought in your head."
Chuckle, say, to caregivers who insert them in wrong
  ears
or not at all. Then, hearing aids lost three times
and each time a challenge met to replace them,
third time with the help of ninety-three-year-old
Korean War-era vet Bob, his breakfast buddy
from Tee Jaye's.
"But what does it matter? He has dementia,"
one memory care aide says.

Two decades ago, he fought wearing them, said "never
again," but again's a rerun. Wife's fight
wins with urgent planning
searches, gets 1950s paperwork in order for VA, after his
  May
dementia diagnosis. "They say I'm losing my marbles,"
he jokes, humors wife when she does all heavy work
for a new set—just $50 for an army vet, when

twenty years before, he claims hearing aids a rip-off,
worthless apparatus. $3000 down the drain,
the cliché he espoused, when all
he did was try them on once, did not go back for an

adjustment, and didn't get an office call after the
    spectacle
he made with shouts of "I can hear clearly!" pacing back
and forth, flailing arms about the shocked room.
"Sitting me there is the electric chair," he points with
middle finger, then

newest arrives late summer and cause for
celebration. Wife inserts in his ears,
pictures taken by third daughter at every angle
then the next month, four months from his first
diagnosis, wife passes. Photos become examples
for daughters, for home caregivers, for aides
in assisted living, now memory care, if they
remember to look at them, first displayed in tandem

with signs with arrows that remind
about his clothes sets, his belts
always in place, always in the same space, just like
the liners for waste cans brought in that are never
    replaced
and labels on each dresser drawer in turquoise paper
alerting aides where socks are, undershirts, pajama pants.
His name, written in every single item because so much
is stolen, and the resident who thinks she manages the
facility walks into his room, inspects, and often leaves
with his underwear. Dementia stretches
its Silly Putty days

and he morphs kinder, more complacent, oddly
ready to wear hearing aids daily, while cognition
wanes. Daughters visit daily. Check. Recheck.
Daughter visits late, finds both hearing aids
in his ears in bed one night, when they should have
been removed, returned to charger box. He shivers
in sleep. She lifts slim blanket, finds him in only

There's a Rock on Martin Avenue

T-shirt and Depends. A claim of no awareness about
sleepwear or all messages surrounding details of his
care, not on their radar. He wakes

mouths hollow *home* with a question mark.
She sings what he sang in her childhood ear
to get her to sleep, hopes for reciprocation:
"Bless this house, O Lord we pray;
make it safe by night and day. Amen."

Now his ashes
wait for transfer
to his memorial. Hearing aid charger box
centers in between holiday branches—
an open nest built from everyone's prayers.

Sandra Feen and Cliff Treyens

Neverland
[Cliff]

After decades of bacon and eggs, hot coffee, and side orders of boisterous chatter, belly laughs, and life's laments, the Wednesday Morning Breakfast Club may be nearing its end. It seems the ravages of age have taken their toll.

One week at the end of 2023, only Ray, 100, was in his usual seat along with Sandy and me, young'uns in our sixties. Dementia is a cruel adversary, whittling away at and eventually taking Vern and Wilma four days apart in November, 2023. Of the men, only Bob and Steve are left.

For me, this is cause for reflection.

An ancient perspective on life and aging is just as apt today as it was when Israel's King Solomon wrote it nearly three millennia ago. Known throughout history as a man of wisdom, Solomon penned Ecclesiastes as part of his contribution to the Bible's wisdom.

In Ecclesiastes, Solomon reflects on the cycles of life and their predictability in the refrain, "There is nothing new under the sun." He observes that in the end it seems all to be folly, vanity, and striving after the wind—and then you die.

Solomon describes metaphorically the inevitable deleterious effects of old age: "The watchmen of the house tremble (arms, hands) . . . mighty men stoop . . . grinding ones (teeth) stand idle because they are few . . . those who look through the windows (eyes) grow dim . . . the doors on the street (ears) are shut as the sound of the grinding mill is low . . . men are afraid of a high place and of terrors on the road (falling) . . . the grasshopper (old person) drags himself along . . . ."

Solomon muses, "Remember also your Creator in the days of your youth, before the evil days come and the years draw near when you will say, 'I have no delight in them.'"

We see these truths coming home to roost in our little breakfast clutch around that big, round, increasingly empty wooden table at the end of a front room in Tee Jaye's.

Yet, for the longest time, perhaps longer than we dared hope, the Breakfast Club had been like Peter Pan's Neverland, where no one (or the talk) ever grew old. The infirmities were irrelevant—not because they didn't exist, but they didn't matter. For a brief time, once a week, this cadre of codgers were frisky, quick-witted folk who jousted, philosophized, pondered, and spoke kindly when it was most needed.

So here's a toast to the members of the Wednesday Morning Breakfast Club:

To Vern, a man who loved knowledge as well as baseball, devoured more books than food, and detested silly talk; who, as his dementia progressed, morphed from a crusty teacher and finger-wagging lecturer to a cuddly Pooh

Bear; a faithful husband and provider and progenitor of lovely daughters; and a fine human being with a touch of the divine. Vern is the only man I know other than Jesus who had a shrine erected in his honor for his good deeds.

To Bob, a soft-spoken and gentle man, and the only superman I know who has actually gone faster than a speeding bullet; a faithful friend always ready to help someone in need; a storyteller nonpareil; a patriot; a devoted husband and beloved family man; a lover of hot wood fires and warm chocolate chip cookies; a motor coach-driving and jet-flying wheelman who's traversed our country and the world; and lackey to no one, including Chuck Yeager.

To Steve, who never takes guff from anyone; knows more about shoes than Buster Brown and Johnston & Murphy combined; a veritable legend in his own mind . . . er, time; a rough, tough, cream puff wrapped around wife Jeanette's little finger; also a devoted husband and family man; a Tar Heel who's lived life large; a reservoir of country yarns; by his own admission a brawler, sports legend, and knower of all things. When it comes to Steve, as the saying goes, you can't live with him and you can't live without him.

To Ray, patriarch of the Breakfast Club if there can be such a thing among old men; who never saw a breakfast he didn't like; who humbly viewed his life as unremarkable; who rarely had a complaint about anything or anyone; who survived one of the most dangerous jobs in World War II; who worked long, hard hours for forty years to faithfully provide for his family; a model of faithfulness to his sons; a pseudo-stoic who teared up every time he talked about his beloved, departed wife Jean; and an all-around, stand-up guy the kind of which you'd want to have your back.

To Wilma, who was never at a loss for words; a dancer and romancer; Phyllis Diller and Roseanne Barr all rolled into one; an escape artist without peer; a color palette personified; one to keep her kindness a secret as if it would tarnish her image; a self-described tomboy; a righter-of-wrongs; a repo man when it came to retrieving Vern's stolen possessions; and beloved wife, mother, and grandma.

And to an incomplete list of others who participated over the years: John, a kind, gentle, faithful friend who spent countless hours driving his buddies to and from breakfast; Rudy, who narrowly escaped Nazi's Hitler Youth for his beloved, adopted United States of America; David, a retired southern Ohio iron worker who delighted us and vexed Steve with his countrified quirkiness and nonsensical non sequiturs; and Don Moore, one of the most likeable guys you'd ever meet, full of life, who loved to dance, and was known to hum Sinatra tunes.

There are more who preceded my time and contributed greatly to this breakfast club tradition that has proliferated in towns and cities across America and the world as long as older men have been eating food.

God knows how many hours all these men (and Wilma) spent supping together. A cynical person might question whether there could have been something more fruitful to do with their time. Frankly, I resisted the group, but I became fair game upon retirement.

I would take issue with the cynics. Wise as he was, Solomon wasn't entirely right when he said ". . . evil days come and the years draw near when you will say, 'I have no delight in them.'" Solomon should have been so lucky as to take a place at the Breakfast Club table.

Sandra Feen and Cliff Treyens

Acknowledgments

Grateful acknowledgment is given to the following publications in which these poems first appeared, sometimes in a slightly different form.—Sandra Feen

National and International Beat Poetry Foundation Anthology, 2022–Goddess: Poets Celebrating Women (New Generation Beat Publications)—Into the Season

National and International Beat Poetry Foundation Anthology, 2024–Honoring Women (New Generation Beat Publications)—Ash Monday

Border Beats: Writing Across Boundaries (Border Beat Books, 2023)—Easier to Swallow

Poem of the Week at BeatLife.org (12/16/2024)—Easier to Swallow

Cover Photo

Photo taken by Sandra Feen

Much gratitude to Kevin Havens for his excellent graphic work on the cover.

There is a plaque on the rock that reads

Near this spot June 21, 1813
was held a council between
General William Henry Harrison
and the Indians comprising

*Wyandots, Delawares,
Shawnees and Senecas with
Tarhe the Crane
as spokesman resulting in
permanent peace
with the Indians of Ohio*

*Erected by the Columbus chapter
Daughters of the American Revolution
June 21, 190*

Immense gratitude to Dianne Borsenik for her
meticulous, exemplary care in reading our manuscript.

Authors' Biographies

Sandra Feen is a member of the Ohio Poetry Association and the Bistro Poets writing critique group. She served as the 2022–2024 Ohio Beat Poet Laureate, and currently co-hosts the monthly online creative arts interview show *The Muse's Mic* with James Bryant.

A member of the poetry troupe *Concrete Wink* with Rikki Santer and Chuck Salmons, Feen's first photography show became intrinsic to their *Winks, Drinks and Vibes* reading, held at the Sunbear Studio in Westerville, Ohio, in February, 2022. *Concrete Wink* wrote ekphrastic poems to two dozen of her photos on display. In addition, she has read in venues in and out of Ohio for over thirty years. She also read at Connecticut's National Beat Poetry Festival and New York's Brooklyn Poets Yawp, and she performed work by Holocaust writers in Susan Millard Schwartz's *Anahata Music Project*. She has participated in many online poetry activities, including several podcasts.

Feen has given poetry therapy workshops throughout Ohio and has seventy hours toward certification. She has a BFA in Creative Writing and a BS in English Education from Bowling Green State University, as well as an MA in Literature from Wright State University. She was one of twelve teachers selected for a National

Endowment of the Arts first *Change Course* program through Wright State University's Institute on Writing and Its Teaching. She has taught adult evening high school English courses, including Drama, and worked as a proofreader for a braille textbook company.

Feen's work has been published in numerous anthologies and journals, and she is the author of *Evidence of Starving* (Voice Lux Journal, 2021) *Meat and Bone* (Luchador Press, 2019), and *Fragile Capacities: School Poems* (NightBallet Press, 2018). *Fragile Capacities*, which was nominated for the Ohioana Book Award, highlights her thirty-two-year teaching career in Columbus City Schools. Her poem "Palms Monday" was nominated for a Pushcart Prize.

In 2008, she traveled with her childhood friend, Debra, to the Jimmy Carter Peace Center and they had their pictures taken with Roselyn and Jimmy Carter. At a reception, Jimmy Carter approached Sandy, put his hand on her shoulder, and while squeezing it, said "Did you get enough to eat, young lady?"

Cliff Treyens began his writing career as a gradeschooler scrawling fantastical stories about space ships and such. After a brief stint on his high school newspaper, he majored in journalism at Ohio State University. Upon graduation in 1977, he worked twenty months at the *Valley News Dispatch* in New Kensington, Pennsylvania.

From there, Treyens moved to *The Clarion-Ledger* in Jackson, Mississippi, where he became a Statehouse reporter and part of a reporting team that won the 1983 Pulitzer Prize for Distinguished Public Service. *The Clarion-Ledger's* entry included fifty-one news stories and twenty-seven editorials detailing problems in Mississippi's system of public education. Due to the public pressure for change, the Mississippi Legislature passed an historic education reform act designed to address many of the state's public education deficiencies.

In October 1985, Treyens moved back to his hometown of Columbus, Ohio, to serve two years as a Statehouse reporter for the *The Columbus Dispatch*, then back to Jackson, Mississippi, to be the Director of Communications for Governor Ray Mabus. It was with Governor Mabus (who later became President Obama's Secretary of the Navy for eight years) that Treyens' writing capabilities greatly expanded to include speech writing, script writing, and acerbic writing to contentious reporters. Treyens returned to Columbus in 1991 to work for Ohio House Speaker Vern Riffe as his communications director. Following Riffe's retirement, Treyens assisted Riffe with *Whatever's Fair: The Political Autobiography of Ohio House Speaker Vern Riffe,* which was published by The Kent State University Press in 2007. Treyens finished out his working career with fifteen years at the National Ground Water Association as Director of Public Awareness.

Throughout his life, he has had the occasion to meet or interview President Lyndon Johnson, Jesse Owens, Rosa Parks, President Ronald Reagan, Jesse Jackson, Muhammad Ali, Arnold Schwarzenegger, Congressman John Lewis, and John Grisham.

Treyens says his most significant labor, by far, has been being a follower of Jesus Christ. He looks forward to spending eternity pursuing the infinitely fascinating, challenging, and rewarding goal of loving God, and of loving people.

There's a Rock on Martin Avenue

www.ingramcontent.com/pod-product-compliance
Lightning Source LLC
Chambersburg PA
CBHW050522100526
44581CB00002B/76